Spontaneous Drama
A Language Art

Spontaneous Drama
A Language Art

John W. Stewig

The University of Wisconsin
at Milwaukee

Charles E. Merrill Publishing Company
A Bell & Howell Company
Columbus, Ohio

Published by
Charles E. Merrill Publishing Co.
A Bell & Howell Company
Columbus, Ohio 43216

Copyright © 1973 by Bell & Howell Company. All rights reserved. No part of this book may be reproduced in any form, electronic or mechanical, including photocopy, recording, or any information storage and retrieval system, without permission in writing from the publisher.

International Standard Book Number: 0-675-09009-1

Library of Congress Catalog Card Number; 72-91801

1 2 3 4 5 6 7 8 9 10—77 76 75 74 73

Printed in the United States of America

To Eleanor

*for living her belief that
we can become more than we are*

Preface

Have you tried doing drama with the children in your classroom? If you are among the small number who have, did the experience make you want to do it more often? Many teachers have heard about dramatics for children, but balk at the idea of trying it because drama in the classroom is so different from more conventional academic activities. Perhaps you've not tried leading children in informal drama experiences simply because what you knew of drama was too unclear to you. Or, perhaps you have not known *what* to do or *why* you should do it.

The purpose of this book is to convince you, as I am convinced, that all children should have regular experiences in spontaneous drama in the classroom. This book is for you, the classroom teacher, whether you have been teaching many years or are only now approaching the student-teaching experience. It was written as a result of my six years of elementary school teaching and my conviction that you *can* learn how to do drama with children. All that really is necessary is a desire to learn and a belief in the values of drama, which frees children to express their ideas.

The book's focus is on spontaneous drama, a vehicle for encouraging, extending, and enhancing the creativity children bring to your classroom. It spells out in detail the growth in language creativity which results when children work with a teacher who provides informal drama experiences. The book details carefully *what* spontaneous dramatics is, *how* it is done with children, and *why* it should be a part of the elementary curriculum. In addition, the book includes a step-by-step sample sequence of improvised drama experiences to show you how to put to use the theoretical ideas in actual sessions with children in your class room. Finally, the book includes an annotated list of materials valuable for motivating drama.

All of this has been done with one idea in mind—to encourage teachers, including those who have never had drama experience, to set boldly forth on an experiment with their children. When teacher and children work together in improvised drama, important social, intellectual, and emotional goals can be attained. An important natural resource —children's creativity—can receive the encouragement it deserves. As a teacher concerned with human resources, you can do something.

I would like to thank Mrs. Anne Thurman and Miss Dawn Murray of the drama department of the Evanston, Illinois, public schools for many hours of patient labor in reading the manuscript and making myriad helpful suggestions.

John W. Stewig

Contents

1 Introduction and Definitions   1
2 The "What" of Spontaneous Drama   16
3 The "How" of Spontaneous Drama   40
4 Drama as a Language Art   75
5 A Suggested Sequence of Spontaneous Dramatics   101
6 Reference Lists   143
   Index   161

1

Introduction and Definitions

The little boy, in no way good looking, too large for his grade—therefore, gawky—was memorable only for the amount of disruption he caused in the class. Yet, as we worked over the course of several weeks through a sequence of experiences in drama, I thought I detected some changes. The loud voice was at times less penetrating, and the impulses to act the clown or to misbehave for attention seemed less frequent.

Yet it was not until the day we began work on *The King with Six Friends*[1] that the changes became clearly apparent. The class was divided into several small groups in order to involve each child, because the story has only nine characters. We worked on interpretations of the story, and then redid them so the children could be different characters. Tom, who previously had been usually on the edge of the group, was chosen to be king in one group this time. When his group shared its interpretation with the rest of us, the way in which Tom had become the king was striking. In bearing and demeanor, in voice and every action, he portrayed for us the regal monarch. Later that day, as we were walking out to recess, he came up beside me and confided shyly that the real reason he liked drama was "... because everybody gets to be king."

Something in the series of spontaneous drama experiences we had been doing touched this child, drawing out of him some qualities of which the class and I were unaware. The experiences had not "taught" him anything—in the conventional sense of the word. He had learned no new facts or memorized no new dates. But he, indeed, had learned some things about himself and his relations to others which affected his

---

[1] Jay Williams (New York: Parents' Magazine Press, 1968). This is a delightful story of the unusual friends the deposed King meets on his journey, which results in his happy marriage after many adventures.

behavior in positive ways. He came to an understanding of himself as a contributing member of the group, needing to be neither withdrawn nor aggressive to be accepted.

This is only *one* example of *one* way in which children can grow through continued contacts with spontaneous drama. There are many other ways, and we will be exploring them in this book. But in order to understand what drama can do for children, we first need to understand the nature of drama, and more specifically, spontaneous drama.

Drama, an ancient art form, shares one characteristic with all the other arts. All art forms, whether it be painting, sculpture, dance, writing, or drama, are alike in that they are the artist's individual reaction to a stimulus. These individual expressions or comments made by the artists take different outward forms but share the unique quality of being a response to or a statement about something the artist felt was important. The painter sees an arrangement of objects and creates a still life. The writer contemplates an aspect of human nature and fashions a story about someone whose personality embodies this trait. The dramatist observes a recurrent human problem and writes a play in which the characters deal with this problem.

In all these instances, when the public finally sees the art, it is in finished form. By the time a painting is hung in a gallery, the artist's work is finished. By the time the playgoer reaches the theatre, the playwright's work is finished. Drama—meaning a play—is a polished form. This is in contrast to *spontaneous drama,* an art form for children which emphasizes process instead of product. In spontaneous drama, children use their bodies and voices to create a response to a stimulus material. The motivation may be visual, aural, or related to another sense. The child is required to create a response of his own, to create a personal reaction to the stimulus material.

An educator of much perception, whose career is devoted to using drama techniques with teenaged delinquent boys, summarizes a major concern of spontaneous drama.

> A great deal of education is concerned basically with putting something into the child's mind, with storing facts, and making it memorize and retain. . . . But surely this "putting in" side of education is only a part of the matter and should be subsidiary to the development outwards of the child's personality and character from within the child himself.[2]

Putting in or taking out, which shall it be? As with all dichotomies, this one is artificial. Surely no one vitally concerned with educating children would seriously argue that *all* of education should be either cramming ideas in or pulling them out. However, there is danger that

---

[2]Gabriel Barnfield, *Creative Dramatics in Schools* (New York: Hart Publishing Co. 1968), p. 14.

many people—perhaps too many—see the former as the most crucial aspect of education. This is in spite of the fact that people who have studied children have produced powerful statements about the significant work children can do if motivated successfully to draw upon their inner resources.

Over thirty years ago a gifted master teacher (who happened to lack a "proper" degree in teaching) wrote a compelling book describing how she freed children to produce expressive art, music, dance, and writing, using very simple motivations.[3] The book is one of the few in education which is well worth reading despite its advanced age.

Perhaps the reason why Natalie Robinson Cole's newest book[4] seems so pertinent today to those of us interested *first* in children's welfare and then in teaching them academic subjects is that so much of what she wrote over thirty years ago is still waiting to be put into effect by teachers.

Why Is Drama a Language Art?

The title of this book asserts that spontaneous dramatics is one of the language arts. Perhaps to be more accurate it should read that dramatics *should* be part of the language arts program. To understand why this contention is made, one must examine the nature of language arts programs in the elementary school.

A curious aspect of these programs is that their emphasis is somewhat out of touch with the way people use language as adults. To support this statement, we need to be aware of the nature of both adult use of language and language arts programs.

Linguists have long pointed out the primacy of oral language, i.e., the importance of speech. Most adults use language orally, whether they are a college methods professor leading a class discussion or an automobile mechanic discussing with his service manager the reason for performing a particular repair. For the majority of us, we use—*most* of the time—whatever oral proficiency we have developed. A look at elementary language arts programs, however, reveals that this proficiency generally is not true of these programs.

Language arts programs have become so codified it is not impossible to predict what a program might be like without ever visiting the classroom or talking with the teacher. Most frequently the teacher will be using one of the nationally distributed hard-back basic language

---

[3]N.R. Cole, *The Arts in the Classroom* (New York: The John Day Co. 1941). An interesting aspect of this book is that it is one of the first dealing with methods of working with children from "disadvantaged" backgrounds. Cole, who worked in southern California with children of Mexican-American background, displays an enviable empathy for her children.

[4]N.R. Cole, *Children's Arts from Deep Down Inside* (New York: The John Day Co. 1966)

texts from a major publisher. How he will use this depends upon a variety of elements within his classroom: his interest in the book, his students' response to it, the amount of time devoted to language arts, and the available supplementary materials. Quite frequently he also will be using a spelling book which ranges in approach from a rather traditional story or interest-topic approach to a more innovative linguistically organized one. Somewhat less frequently he will be giving either cursory or compulsive attention to one of the many handwriting series.

You'll notice that in the foregoing description *oral* language, the most important facet of language, is absent. It is difficult to find in the proliferating splendidness of basic materials for a language arts program some which relate specifically to the oral arts—listening and speaking.

Several writers have commented on the need to develop sequential programs in listening,[5] oral language,[6] and dramatics,[7] but little has been accomplished in these areas. It is these areas, and the speech skills so crucial to most adult speakers, that are, paradoxically, most frequently ignored in elementary language arts programs.

Further, while it is true that most children do get some experiences in oral language in primary grades (e.g., show-and-tell period), it is rather limited. Regular dramatic experiences are almost never a part of the on-going language arts program.

Because of the widespread view among linguists that language is primarily a spoken art, language programs which do not give children chances to talk should be viewed by teachers as inadequate. It is my contention that the addition of spontaneous dramatics to the language arts curriculum can provide the necessary opportunities for development of language and language-related abilities. Some of the specific language skills which dramatics develop are discussed later in the book.

Components of Drama

All spontaneous drama experiences are made up of four basic components, which will be introduced briefly here and explained more fully in Chapter 2.

---

[5]Wesley G. Sowards and Mary Margaret Scobey, *The Changing Curriculum and the Elementary Teacher* (Belmont, Calif.: Wadsworth Publishing Co., 1968), pp. 129–135.

[6]Wilma M. Possien, *They All Need to Talk* (New York: Appleton-Century-Crofts, 1969). The author has examined fully, giving many classroom examples, the variety of oral activities which are possible in the elementary school.

[7]Ann Shaw, *A Taxonomy of Objectives in Creative Dramatics* (New York: Columbia University, unpublished Ph.D. dissertation, 1968). This is the first attempt, made quite convincingly, to apply the procedure of writing behavioral objectives to the art form of creative dramatics. People in the arts generally view this approach with skepticism. It will be interesting to see how this attempt is accepted by creative dramatics leaders.

Material. This is the idea which is used to motivate the sessions, the stimulus material around which a session is built. Motivations usually appeal to the senses of the child. They should be open-ended so they provide opportunities for a child to create a response.

Discussion-Questioning Segment. After the leader presents the motivating material, and sometimes as this is going on, discussion occurs. This is spontaneous, i.e., not preplanned by the leader. But it is directed by the leader through his judicious use of questions.

Playing of an Idea. This stage varies in complexity depending on the age and previous drama experience of the children. Sometimes this is a simple pantomime of a single activity, e.g., opening a box containing a birthday present; at other times it is more complex, e.g., playing an entire story which the children have created.

Evaluation. This is an important element in drama experiences because the children are encouraged to consider what they have done and to decide which aspects they were pleased with, and which could have been done more effectively.

These components vary in importance depending on the group of children involved, the ideas used for the drama session, how long the children have been having drama experiences, and the purposes for the particular session. The components will be explained more completely in Chapter 2.

Terminology

There are various terms peculiar to dramatics, especially the drama experiences discussed in this book. The most common title for what this book is about is *creative dramatics,* but even though the term is used by many people concerned with the idea, I purposely avoided it. There are two reasons for this:

1. "Creative" has been so misapplied to such a variety of different phenomena that it is almost impossible to establish a clear, denotative meaning for the word. People bring such a variety of reactions to the term—including some negative ones—that I thought best to avoid the problem by simply not using the term at all.
2. Drama should *always* be creative, so as an adjective, the word creative is redundant. If we accept different types of creativity, then all drama, from the informal dramatic play of pre-school children to the finely disciplined Shakespearean performance

(and including such activities as lighting and scenery construction), is creative.

Another term sometimes used to describe drama experiences with children is *developmental drama*. Used widely by Canadian drama leaders, the term emphasizes the fact that as a child lives with this art form throughout his elementary school years, regularly recurring drama experiences develop abilities in characterization, plot creation, mood and conflict establishment, and other facets of dramatics. This term implies that a leader is present, planning carefully to provide for children a sequence of experiences in each of the aspects of dramatics and that through these experiences each child develops that variety of abilities, attitudes, outlooks, and understandings which come from a sustained contact with drama.

However, for this book the emphasis is slightly different, since the dramatic activities are described as *spontaneous*. This is intentional in order to point out the absolute essentiality of an intuitive, flexible, adapting, and dramatic experience which is truly spontaneous. A dictionary lists natural, which is a good word to describe the drama experience we are considering here, as one synonym for spontaneous. Leaders are concerned with evoking in children a natural or spontaneous response to the chosen motivation. This is akin to the free, unstructured response of young children's imaginative play, so respected in the nursery and so quickly discouraged in first grade.

The leader does not formulate ahead of time what the children's response to the material ought to be, but rather plans a motivation and then builds a dramatic experience as the children's natural responses to that motivation come forth. This use of this term does not, however, mean that the drama *program* is spontaneous or unplanned.

Earlier in this century there were several variations of the belief held by some educators in this country that programs in elementary schools should evolve from the needs of the children; that is, the curriculum should be *emergent* and the major role of the teacher should be to follow the expressed interests of the children.[8] People who held this philosophy did not believe that the teacher should present an idea in order to stimulate an interest, but rather he should help children to study something after an interest was expressed.

---

[8]Caroline Pratt, *I Learn From Children* (New York: Simon and Schuster, 1948). This is a delightful account of the work of a courageous and innovative educator who experimented with many "progressive" ideas, among them an *emergent* curriculum. Though now primarily of historical interest, the book does demonstrate conclusively the benefits to be gained from this approach to curriculum planning. (Now out of print, but probably available in public libraries.)

This is not the role of the spontaneous drama leader. Many writers on the nature of the creative act have pointed out that children cannot create in a vacuum,[9] but must be exposed to some sort of stimulus. So the role of the drama leader is one of locating and selecting from among the available materials the ones which he thinks will be most effective in accomplishing his particular purpose for the session. This requires preplanning, but not of the entire lesson.

Another term widely used throughout this book is *leader*. I use this term because for too many teachers, and people preparing to be teachers, the role for which the word "teacher" stands is largely a didactic one, mainly occupied with the dispensing of information. Though there is no dictionary that says the role of the teacher is that standing in front of a group of children and talking *at* them, this is a too common picture, among those in the profession and those outside it. This is not a role congruent with the goals of spontaneous drama. Becoming a spontaneous drama leader requires some abilities different from those you customarily use when teaching more conventional subject matter. These differences should become more apparent later in the book.

Throughout the book I will be talking about spontaneous drama *sessions,* another purposeful change in terminology. This is used to avoid calling them lessons, for far too many people bring negative connotations to the word "lesson." Alice and her friends, in their discussion of lessons, illustrate this problem for us.

"We had the best of educations—in fact, we went to school every day—" . . .

"And how many hours a day did you do lessons?" said Alice.

"Ten hours the first day," said the Mock Turtle: "nine the next, and so on."

"What a curious plan." exclaimed Alice.

"That's the reason they're called lessons," the Gryphon remarked: "because they lessen from day to day."

This was quite a new idea to Alice, and she thought it over a little before she made her next remark. "Then the eleventh day must have been a holiday?"

"Of course it was," said the Mock Turtle.

"And how did you manage on the twelfth?" Alice went on eagerly.

---

[9]Maurie Applegate, *When the Teacher Says Write a Poem and When the Teacher Says Write a Story* (Scranton, Pa.: Harper & Row, 1965). The opinion about the necessity of triggering creativity is widely held; perhaps it is as well expressed by Applegate as by anyone. Several of her books about writing are of interest, though they are not directly related to dramatics activities.

8   Introduction and Definitions

"That's enough about lessons," the Gryphon interrupted in a very decided tone.[10]

The idea of lessons becoming shorter is pleasant to many people, for unfortunately too many students have been convinced that lessons are something unpleasant, to be endured until escape is possible. Thus, instead of lessons, we refer to drama sessions. There are two other reasons:

1. There is not a specific "chunk" of material which must be covered in a given time span, whether that span be a single session, a month's experience, or a year's work. The teacher does have a plan, but as will be pointed out later, this must remain flexible so that adjustments can be made as the session progresses. A higher degree of flexibility must be present than is usually possible in more academic lessons, the learning dimensions of which are all too frequently established by curriculum planners, subject matter experts, textbook writers, and the teacher in the grade higher than the one you teach.[11]

2. The mental "set" of both leader and students is different from that in a conventional academic lesson where children too frequently "take in" whatever is presented. Admittedly, in a drama session the leader is presenting something, but only for the purpose of motivating the children; there is no intent that they should remember details in the material. Confronted with a visual image, an aural message, or a tactile sensation, children are expected to engage in a process of drawing from within themselves responses and reaction, selecting the most appropriate of these, and playing them out while interacting with other children who are doing the same thing. If, after using the material in a session, children do remember details of names, occurrences, and sequences, this is a dividend—not the purpose of the session.

Interpreting Versus Improvising

To some the term improvising may seem a cumbersome way to say "act out." Frequently teachers respond to ideas in dramatics by saying, "But I do that all the time in my reading classes." However, there is a rather subtle distinction between *interpreting* a story and *improvising* one.

[10]Lewis Carroll, *Alice's Adventures In Wonderland and Through the Looking-Glass* (London: J. M. Dent and Sons, Ltd. New York: E. P. Dutton & Co., 1954), pp. 82–84.

[11]Helen Heffernan, "Language Arts Programs in Elementary Schools" in *Guiding Children's Language Learning*, ed. Pose Lamb (DuBuque, Iowa: William C. Brown, 1971), pp. 39–72. In this chapter Miss Heffernan clearly describes the dilemma of the classroom teacher trying to meet requirements imposed from outside and yet attempting to fashion a program appropriate to his children.

It is, of course, true that many elementary school teachers make extensive use of interpreting literature in their reading classes. This takes many forms. It may vary from simply assigning certain children to read each of the character parts in the current story to allowing a group to enact the story without using the book as a cuecard. In these activities a crucial element is successful and accurate interpretation, enactment, or re-creation of the author's statement and intent.

For example, in working with "The Fox and the Grapes,"[12] when a teacher talks with children about how they can convey the anger of the thwarted fox and what sounds and bodily movements they can utilize to show this, he is still in essence working with interpreting, not improvising.

However, when he faces the children, perhaps after simple enactment as described above, and asks, "Can you imagine what might have happened if the grapes *had* fallen into the fox's paws?" *then* he is asking the children to extend, to extrapolate, to enrich the basic materials with ideas of their own making. This, then, is the point at which one moves from interpreting to improvising and begins to do spontaneous drama with children.

Perhaps another example will clarify the distinction. Allowing children to choose parts and read a story as they want is doubtlessly valuable. In such a story as the *Midas Touch*,[13] children revel in impersonating the greedy king and his pathetic daughter. But, the "typical" teacher, even though he may sense that the children are learning from such an experience, would probably move to more practical considerations; the results of such impersonation wouldn't be tangible enough for him.

Creative improvisation is the major emphasis in spontaneous dramatics. It is defined here as being entirely different than interpretation, as it involves going *beyond* the basic material. Taking the theme of the *Midas Touch* story, there are a variety of possible questions to which children could easily respond:

1. Why do you imagine the king was so greedy? What might have made him this way?
2. How did his daughter happen to be so sweet, having been raised alone in the castle with her father as an example?

---

[12] *Aesop's Fables* (New York: Golden Press, 1966), p. 23. This collection, selected and adapted by Louis Untermeyer, is particularly useful. The book is large and lavishly illustrated by the Provensens, who have done their usual superb job of capturing the essence of the material and yet providing a unique visual experience for their readers.

[13] While many reading series include this myth, if you decide to use it in drama you may consult Olivia Coolidge, *Greek Myths* (Boston: Houghton Mifflin, 1949), pp. 90–100. It contains a wealth of informative details often omitted in simpler versions.

3. How did the king react to other people? (You will recall that in the story we do not see him interacting with other people.) What do you think he was like to his servants? The people of the town?
4. In what other ways could he have solved his problem?

Children would enjoy improvising these ideas. The teacher might use some of these questions to stimulate discussion, others to encourage children to "act out" their responses and to create *other* episodes which could occur before, during, and after the basic story.

No matter what specific questions the teacher uses to begin a session, he easily could move from interpretation to improvisation and provide an experience in spontaneous drama for his children. In essence he would ask the children to draw from within themselves ideas, thoughts, feelings, and conclusions based on, but not found in, the basic material.

Another example, on the college rather than elementary school level, illustrates the essential difference between the processes. Recently while working with a group of students on the poem "The Sandhill Crane" (found on page 115 in Chapter 5), we were thinking together about the words and at one point were examining what ideas the word "scuttle" brought to our minds. We tried scuttling, some on stomachs stretched flat on the floor, some as small four-legged animals moving rapidly in the way the word suggested to them. Soon one of the students commented that minnows wouldn't scuttle in many different directions, but would rather travel in a school until something made them "scuttle away in fear," as the poem describes it. Another girl suggested that she could be a stone, and another student could throw her into the midst of the school of fish. This idea appealed to the group, and so they formed a compact school and swam on their stomachs across the room until the girl who was the stone was thrown into their midst. Then such a scuttling was seen! They had developed the idea beautifully, and in addition, provided an example of how to build an incident spontaneously. None of this was included in the poem; the minnow is only one of the small animals mentioned incidentally by the poet as she built upon the idea of fear. Yet, since our goal was not simply literal interpretation of what was there, but rather *improvisation*, which is the essence of spontaneous dramatics, we decided that it was well worth the time to act out the scuttle incident. The same students began to create ideas based on the poem but not found in it, as they saw there were endless suggestions within the bounds of this simple poem, as is indeed the case with any bit of motivational material.

Dramatics Is Not Theatre

One aspect of creative or improvisational drama must be emphasized at this point. Though dramatics may lead into creative theatre by children, it is a completely separate entity. There should be no intent, for example, that simple improvisation on a new ending for a favorite fairy tale lead into a fully costumed and lighted adaptation of a scripted play for parents. Children may eventually mature from simple spontaneous creation of a new character in the story *Stone Soup*[14] to authorship of a new version of *Cinderella*. But if such does occur, it must happen because of the children's desire to do so. The leader, in fact, must be constantly wary that he succumbs neither to his own need or those of the principal or PTA president to mount a production for an audience.

In the landmark film done by Rita Crist,[15] the group does evolve a semi-finished play based on the poem introduced by the leader. When this happens naturally, as an expression of interest by the children, there are additional learnings which occur as the sessions progress in this direction. It is, however, imperative that the leader continually examine his motivations to make sure that it is the children's, and not his own, ideas which are making a more formal "play" seem important.

Qualities of Spontaneous Drama

There are several qualities of spontaneous drama which are unique. As in the case of other sections in this chapter, a brief introduction will be given here and more complete explanations in Chapter 2.

Spontaneous drama is *inclusive*. This means that all children can participate. Because the emphasis is not on preparing finished productions for performance, all children in your group should be encouraged to take part, regardless of the amount of "skill" or lack of it which they show.

Spontaneous drama is *on-going*. The drama leader does have a purpose in mind for each session he plans, but because the emphasis in dramatics is on the *process* and not on the *product*, if a particular purpose is not accomplished in one session, it may be accomplished in a later session.

---

[14]Marcia Brown's illustrations of this old tale (New York: Charles Scribner's Sons, 1947) lend a clearly defined aura of the "strange country" in which the story is set.

[15]*Creative Drama: The First Steps*, 29-minute, sound and color film by Northwestern University Films. Representative episodes selected from an entire sequence of drama sessions, they show in condensed form the procedures for providing children with a variety of drama experiences leading to a rather formal playing of a poem.

Spontaneous drama is *recurring*. Several elements prevail during all drama experiences, whether they involve kindergarten children ferociously stomping around their room as monsters or a group of teenagers tensely enacting a problem presented by drug use. In drama, participants work at varying times with mood, plot, characterization, rhythm, and unity. These drama elements are of concern no matter what the stimulus material may be.

Spontaneous drama is a *process*. While there are some definite, though different, advantages to be gained from involving children of any age in informal play production, the drama leader is aware that this process is unlike the spontaneous drama process. Emphasis in spontaneous drama is on the children being involved in expressing their reaction to a stimulus material, not on presenting something finished for an audience.

Drama and Spontaneous Drama

The chart on page 13 summarizes some of the major distinctions between the two related but different art forms we have been considering.

Values of Dramatics

Many other writers have described effectively and at some length the social and emotional values which accrue when children do drama on a regular basis.[16] Almost any of the books I mention include a rationale for establishing dramatics as part of a child's education. An early pacesetter, Geraldine Siks'[17] book presents a very readable, convincing statement of the values of drama and should be studied simply for the humane approach it expresses and the confidence in children which it exudes. Sadly, this consummate belief in the ability of children to draw ideas from within themselves is not universal among people who teach. The grade-oriented college students we encounter in classes are unwitting witnesses to elementary school experiences with teachers too often more interested in "putting in" rather than in "drawing out."

While the Siks' book is one of several basic books dealing with creative drama, it is mentioned because the author describes at length

---

[16] A particulary helpful list of references is included in James Hoetker, *Dramatics and the Teaching of Literature* (Champaign: National Council of Teachers of English, 1969), pp. 17–44. For those who are interested, the chapter also includes a capsule history of the creative drama movement in the United States.

[17] Geraldine Brain Siks, *Creative Dramatics: An Art for Children* (New York: Harper & Row, 1958).

	Scripted Drama	Spontaneous Drama
Involvement	A few children can be involved, the rest must take backstage or other supportive jobs.	Involves all children in a variety of active roles.
Creativity encouraged	Close adherence to the script by the playwright is manditory.	Children use story or other motivation as a springboard for their own creation.
Pressure to perform	High; children know audience is watching, done in surroundings with which child is often unfamiliar.	Low; if audience exists at all, it is small group of children's peers in the classroom situation with which they are familiar.
Need for props and equipment	Quite extensive; often these are not things children can create, but must be made for them by others.	Minimal or nonexistant; child uses creative imagination to evoke needed equipment, emphasis on refining movements (e.g., picking up a fork) to convey ideas.
Language learnings	Few; children are limited to understanding the uses the author has made of language.	Many; the situations presented challenge children to creative use of language, both verbal and nonverbal.

the following values which children develop when they are involved in a drama program:

1. Confidence and the ability to express themselves creatively.
2. Positive social attitudes and relationships.
3. Emotional stability.
4. Bodily coordination.
5. A philosophy of life (wonderment about their individual ways of living).

14 Introduction and Definitions

For a complete and wider view of dramatics, you should also do some background reading in the other books which are recommended in Chapter 6.

The child's *creativity* can be developed by exposure to drama as has been explained previously. Several people have called for the need for encouraging creativity,[18] have identified the means of doing so,[19] and have described the conditions necessary for encouraging creativity.[20]

Another of the social values developed by dramatics is *teamwork*, which is the very heart of drama. As he works with other children, the child learns to modify his ideas, plans, and thoughts as he is exposed to the ideas, plans, and thoughts of others. The teacher works to encourage this interaction, as children discover that the group with candor and impartiality exerts the discipline necessary for effective playing.

Another value often identified with drama is that it provides children with healthy channels for the *expression of emotions*. When working *on* ideas in drama, the child can also work *out* frustrations, fears, and inhibitions which ordinarily must be kept in during more conventional school classes. Seeing that characters in motivational materials share some of his common problems can be encouraging to a child.

The leader is, of course, aware of the necessity to protect a child whose emotional problems are too intense for exposure to the group. The leader should never see himself as a therapist or the drama session as a catharsis or therapy which will help a disturbed child. Drama is considered a language art, and its purpose is to develop communication abilities. While some highly trained psychologists do use role playing (in some ways similar to drama) to achieve therapeutic ends, this is different from informal drama in the classroom. So, if during a session a child reveals that he has severe emotional problems, the leader should work with the school psychologist or other professional personnel in providing individualized help for the child apart from the drama experiences in the classroom.

---

[18]Ryland W. Crary, *Humanizing the School: Curriculum, Development and Theory* (New York: Alfred A. Knopf, 1969), pp. 285–312. In a book refreshingly unlike other curriculum books, Crary, instead of focusing on content which is currently taught, examines such topics as methodological foundations and procedural bases for curriculum improvement. The chapter on the elementary school is provocative, and the chapter on the creative-aesthetic dimension of curriculum is challenging.

[19]George R. Kneller, *The Art and Science of Creativity* (New York: Holt, Rinehart & Winston, 1965). In a brief, readable book Kneller has examined several theories of creativity, the nature of the creative person and the creative process, and the implications of these for the educative process. The list of references is short, but the book is extensively footnoted.

[20]Ruth G. Strickland, *Language Arts in the Elementary School* (Lexington, Mass.: D.C. Heath & Co., 1969), pp. 314–316.

Drama also provides for the development of *reasoning powers,* for as the child analyzes the appropriateness of what has been done in the session, he begins to evaluate, formulate alternatives, and develop the ability to choose the most appropriate of the alternatives.

All of these abilities are crucial, but because they have been so well explicated elsewhere, they will not be developed more fully here. A unique aspect of dramatics—the *language learning* which this art form can foster—is the focus of this book and described in detail in Chapter 2.

Summary

It is hoped that this brief introduction to the nature of spontaneous drama, the terminology involved in describing this art form, and the values children derive from such experiences has interested you in providing drama experiences for your children. The purpose of the next chapter is to detail more completely how you can provide these experiences for children.

2

The "What" of Spontaneous Drama

In ancient Greek tragedies, a character called the Prologue appeared on stage before the play began to describe briefly the action which was to come. The purpose was to capture the attention of the audience, to inform them briefly of what was to follow. In a way, the purpose of Chapter 1 was the same. Now that you have been introduced to spontaneous drama, the purpose of this chapter is to detail more completely some aspects of drama you will need to know in order to lead drama sessions with your children. We shall begin with the components of the drama session.

Components of Spontaneous Drama

The Material

This is what is used to motivate the session. It usually appeals to the senses of the child.

A. The teacher may use part of a story or a poem. He may read such prose selections as "The Heath-Cat"[1] (though probably part of it will be enough). In using prose selections, the leader should always be aware of the need to condense and simplify, for most of these selections are too long to be used in their original form. The leader should pare the

---

[1]included in *One Hundred Favorite Folktales,* chosen by Stith Thompson. (Bloomington: Indiana University Press, 1968), p. 173. This Portugese folk tale, appropriate for older children, is only one from this collection which includes tales from many European countries with an oral folk tradition. Several of them are useful, not only for dramatization, but for vocabulary expansion.

story down to the "bare bones" of the plot to bring it to manageable length for playing. Or the teacher might use a poem, perhaps like the following one:

SOME ONE[2]

Some one came knocking
  At my wee, small door;
Some one came knocking
  I'm sure-sure-sure;
I listened, I opened,
  I looked to left and right,
But nought there was a-stirring
  In the still dark night;
Only the busy beetle
  Tap-tapping in the wall,
Only from the forest
  The screech-owl's call,
Only the cricket whistling
  While the dew-drops fall,
So I know not who came knocking,
  At all, at all, at all.

B. The leader may use a visual stimulus of some nature, e.g., art reproductions (Walt Kuhn's *White Clown*), objects (a mask borrowed from a historical society or a piece of Mexican sculpture), or photographs, such as the one pictured on the next page taken from Leavitt and Sohn's book.[3]

C. The teacher may use the sense of touch, for example, by having children interpret, through movement, the surface textures of a piece of wood, corduroy, glass, corrugated cardboard, or tweed.

D. The sense of smell could be used by giving the children paper cups filled with such unfamiliar spices as cumin, savory, and chervil, then letting them smell these spices and pantomine their thoughts about

---

[2]from *Peacock Pie,* by Walter de la Mare (New York: Alfred A. Knopf, 1961), p. 12. Reprinted by the permission of The Literary Trustees of Walter de la Mare, and The Society of Authors as their representative. This delightful poem, describing the unexpected caller who didn't wait for the door to be opened, offers rich possibilities for improvisation. The sensitive illustrations by Barbara Cooney add to the usefulness of the book.

[3]Hart Day Leavitt and David A. Sohn, *Stop, Look and Write!* (New York: Bantam Books, 1964). A collection of over 100 dramatic photographs drawn from a variety of cultures, this book is designed to stimulate creative writing. It also includes commentary sections in which the authors suggest ways to help children perceive their world in new ways, and questions to stimulate writing.

18   The "What" of Spontaneous Drama

them. Naturally, actual odors are preferable to imagined ones, and children easily create impromptu scenes built around imagined characters' reactions to olfactory stimulation.

E. Even the sense of taste, perhaps the least utilized avenue of learning in contemporary society, may be used to evoke a dramatic response among children. By taking such a simple taste as that of a lemon, for example, the teacher can give children an opportunity to react.

These, then, are the *sources* of material to which the leader may turn in preparing matter for spontaneous dramatics. But what does he *do* with these basic sources?

The Discussion-Questioning Segment

After exposing the child to the motivation, and indeed sometimes *as* this is going on, discussion occurs—spontaneous, unplanned, but directed by the leader through his questioning.

He may lead off with such questions as the following (keyed to the examples given in the preceding material):

A. Do you have any clues in the poem as to who the caller might have been (page 17)? Do we know anything about the owner of the house? How could this have ended differently—for instance, if the caller had waited?

B. What are some words we could use to describe the expression on the boy's face (page 18)? Does the picture give you some indications of what the situation is? Do the boy's clothes tell you anything about him? Do you get the feeling he may be from another country? Or, do you think the picture may be old?

C. What does the surface of the material feel like (page 17)? Is it regular? If not, do the irregularities form a predictable pattern? By using your body in recurring up and down movements could you represent the contrast between the two levels of the corduroy?

D. What do they smell like (page 17)? Are they pleasant? If so, why? In what sorts of places might you encounter an odor like this? What types of people could be there? What things could they be doing?

E. Who might be tasting this (page 18)? Where could they be? Why might they be alone? What could have happened prior to this to lead the person to want to taste the lemon? What could happen after he tastes the lemon?

In all cases it should be remembered that these are simply sample questions, designed not to be followed prescriptively by a teacher interested in emulating what is described here, but rather only as *examples*. The world is crammed with motivations—each time you are in a different place than you were a half-hour before you're surrounded by new ones. The only problem is to open up yourself to the motivation and develop the ability to ask sensitive questions about it, questions which will help children to open up!

Similarly, there is not *one* right answer to the question. You will notice that, though this book is full of questions, there are no answers provided. This is because the teacher's primary concern is to elicit from children many responses of much variety, to get at the diversity of ideas available when working with children.

The Actual Playing of an Idea

This stage varies greatly, depending upon the age of the children, the amount of experience they have had with drama and their leader has had in directing it, where the lesson happens in the sequence, and the creativity of the children.

Sometimes the children will respond with movement, either representative or abstract. At other times they will pantomine and, with gestures and facial expressions, convey without words a thought or idea. At still other times children will be moved to add dialogue to their playing to supplement the more basic bodily communication.

The above variations are not to be thought of as stages, for, if they are progressive at all, it is only in a very rough way. Though it does appear that dialogue is among the last of the dramatic elements to appear, groups and individuals will make use of one or several of these possibilities at different times, depending both upon the type of motivation used in a particular session and their response to it at a particular moment.

Evaluation

There are basically two different types of evaluation which occur in creative drama: concurrent and terminal.

Concurrent evaluation is of two types, teacher evaluation and group evaluation. As the teacher observes children working, he notes which children are being successful in capturing an idea and conveying it, and so he further encourages the group and individuals by commenting positively as the group works. He may make such general comments as: "My, I see so many dogs, and they *are* being very different," or, "I can really feel the heaviness in your bodies—it comes across well." He may make such specific comments as: "What an effective snake Billy is being," or, "Mary's frog is moving so well."

Group evaluation occurs when the teacher senses a need to consolidate something particularly effective, wants to help the group shift direction, or simply feels the children need a change of pace. He draws the children together, usually in close physical proximity to him to encourage their participation in this transitory quiet period, and they briefly share their reactions to what has been going on. Sometimes he starts the discussion with a very specific question: "What could we do with our legs to make them seem more like a horse's legs?" At other times he asks more general questions: "Did you like what you were doing?" This phase of the session is short—rarely more than a few minutes in length—but it both helps children to return to thinking more analytically about what they have been doing and helps to change directions or make transitions to related but different activities.

Terminal evaluation occurs at the end of each session. On paper this looks like a logical and fairly easy thing to accomplish, but in actual practice it is not so. The leader may find it takes him quite awhile to arrive at the ability of leading this evaluation session, which should be both a summing up of what has been accomplished and of what remains to be accomplished.

Children and leader together discuss what they did which was particularly effective; what was honestly attempted but did not, for one reason or another, turn out to be effective; and what skills, ideas, thoughts, and feelings remain to be worked on at the next session. It must be emphasized that this is not the teacher evaluating the children, but the teacher and children evaluating *together* how the session went.

In both kinds of evaluation, the leader has a short- and long-term purpose. His short-term purpose is to help the children to focus their thinking on the specific action which was taking place, so that they can evaluate it. The long-term purpose is to help them to understand evaluation as a necessary part of spontaneous drama. As he achieves this, the children can move to assuming more and more responsibility for their own evaluation, thus internalizing the procedure and making external encouragement to evaluate less necessary. Children can be brought to the point of evaluating their work by themselves as they participate in an improvisation, but it takes time and expert guidance to develop this rather sophisticated skill.

A Moment to Reflect

The teacher will find it helpful if he can arrange to have a few minutes following the session to make some notes for his own use. If the children can do some work independently for a time, or if the drama period can be set up immediately preceeding the children's scheduled time with one of the special-area teachers, the leader will profit by having a short period of time to review for himself what occurred in the session, and to make some notes about what he wishes to try the next time. Because the session may frequently go in directions other than the planned one, it is desirable to have this time to check plans against outcomes, to assess what was done and what should probably be tried again next time. In my experience, given the pressures faced by most classroom teachers, I find it important to jot these few notes. By the time the next session comes, after an interval of a day or two, aspects of drama which seemed to need attention at the close of the previous session will have faded from sight. Because of this the program will be less effective.

This, then, completes our definition of spontaneous drama. It is children responding to a motivation, sometimes in simple rhythmic movement, at other times in more complex but informal playing of a theme or story. While they experience dramatics, children grow socially, emotionally, rhythmically, and intellectually. In addition, children also increasingly develop competency in oral language. There are four components of the drama sessions: 1) the material, 2) the discussion, 3) the playing of the ideas, and 4) the evaluation. In thinking about these ideas and in the actual working with children, however, the leader must keep in mind the basic premise that drama is drawing out ideas, thoughts, emotions, and reactions from within the child. It is a freeing of the creative impulse children possess.

Qualities of Spontaneous Drama Experiences

The purpose of the first two chapters is to develop a many-sided definition of spontaneous drama. Like any process in which people are involved, a simple definition is impossible. To continue this process of defining, some unique *qualities* of this type of drama will be considered here. These were mentioned briefly in Chapter 1, but may be easier to understand if they are expanded upon.

Inclusive Quality

Perhaps one of the most distinguishing qualities of spontaneous drama, setting it apart from other theatre activities, is its inclusiveness. Opportunity is provided for all children to participate, and the premium is not on the potential Barrymore or Bernhart, but rather on the ability to take an idea and react spontaneously to it. This latter ability is one which most, if not all, children can develop.

The key word in the preceeding paragraph is *opportunity*, for it is crucial that, even with very young children, spontaneous drama be an opportunity, not a requirement. The leader first makes a genuine attempt to involve all children in his group. This includes allowing those timid or unresponsive children to play inanimate objects, if this gives them security. This has happened to me frequently—from the kindergartner who preferred to be a blade of grass when the rest óf us were slithering along on our snake stomachs, to the two college juniors who didn't relate to our poem about animals and preferred to be the dam in the river. Since we were doing "The Sandhill Crane"[4] this seemed like an original idea on their part, so they were encouraged to use it.

Although the leader works diligently to involve all children, he sometimes does not succeed. Since we are attempting to release children's creative potential and *not* simply to add another compulsory subject to the curriculum, it is perfectly acceptable if a child wants to retire to a corner with a book rather than participate. Usually, the eavesdropping begins quickly enough and, seeing others enjoying their involvement, the child chooses to rejoin the group. However, sometimes

---

[4]Mary Austin, "The Sandhill Crane," in *Arbuthnot Anthology of Children's Literature*, by May Hill Arbuthnot (Chicago: Scott, Foresman and Co., 1961), p. 53. The Arbuthnot book is without question one of the basic anthologies of children's literature. It includes the best selections from all genres of literature and these are, as in the case of poetry, arranged conveniently according to subject.

the leader bides his time and waits, but he keeps trying to involve all children, since all children can both contribute to the activity and learn from it.

On-Going Quality

The dramatics leader has a plan for his session. Among less experienced leaders this may be rather carefully written out to detail materials, motivation, procedures, and evaluational techniques. With more experienced leaders this may be more simply an idea of the direction in which he wants to go. In both cases, however, the leader remembers there are other sessions coming later, meaning that, though a session is by no means devoid of purpose, it is also by no means considered a failure if the exact purpose is not reached in that particular session. Providing something of benefit occurred in the session, the leader can be content. He can work with his original idea again later. Perhaps an example will clarify this.

Suppose a leader is working with the idea of mood, using the story of *Little Red Riding Hood*.[5] His main purpose might be to help children to sense the mystery of the forest and how the trees, growing closely together, allow only dimly filtered light to sift through to the narrow and rocky path beneath. Suppose, however, that in attempting to play this idea with children, they become fascinated with the idea of Little Red Riding Hood's character. One group I worked with became concerned with how she could be so gullible, so oblivious to obvious danger signals; so, the group decided to develop a characterization of a slightly more perspicacious Little Red Riding Hood. The devious wolf had a much more difficult job in our adapted version of the folk tale, when Little Red took on some of the sophistication natural to the space-age children who were improvising.

The leader should not be dismayed when deviations from the plan like the above occur. While it is true that he intended to work on mood, it is also true that, because there is no specified material to be "covered," he can have another session on mood later.[6] Children experience curricula established by state commissions, by textbook writers, by local curriculum guides, by expert subject matter authorities—all of which

---

[5]The reader might be interested in using the version included in *Story and Verse for Children*, by Miriam Blanton Huber (New York: The Macmillan Co., 1967), p. 256. This is another large anthology of children's literature which any teacher in the elementary school would find to be an indispensible reference.

[6]Perhaps for variety a second session with this folk tale could be based on Nonny Hogrogian's version in which both granny and the ingenuous Red come to a mournful end. See *The Renowned History of Little Red Riding Hood* (New York: Thomas Y. Crowell Co., 1967).

specify a quantity of materials (X) which must be covered in a quantity of time (Y).

The spontaneous drama program is not contained within the boundaries of X and Y. The leader can, next session perhaps, choose another story. For example, he could use *The Three Bears,*[7] also set in a forest, for work on mood. The leader also is not bound by considerations of "finishing" something by a given time because he tailors the dramatics program as he goes, and he does not rush on to something else, fearing what the teacher next year will expect the children to have learned.

Given the fact that the leader needs to be flexible enough to follow up leads from the children which he may not have anticipated in planning the session, he also attends to the frequency with which this occurs. If children regularly go in directions other than he has planned and accomplish purposes other than he has identified, some examination of his techniques may be in order. The leader should then consider such questions as:

1. Do I have a purpose firmly enough in mind that I could describe it to someone? Or, could I write it out?
2. Have I been careful enough in selecting materials to achieve my purpose? (While it is true that most materials are multi-purpose, it is also true that some are better than others for particular purposes.)
3. Have I been taking enough time to communicate my purpose to the children?

The sensitive leader is flexible enough to change directions, or purpose, during the session. However, he is also aware enough to re-evaluate his own planning and leading techniques if changes happen with regularity.

Recurring Quality

There are certain basic recurring ideas, strands, or organizing elements which pervade dramatics programs at any level. These are *mood, plot, characterization, rhythm,* and *unity.* Because they recur, college juniors, even though they may have been in dramatics programs for quite some time, are as concerned with them as kindergarten children. One exam-

---

[7]Some leaders have found *The Story of the Three Bears* (London: Warne, n.d.) with drawings by L. Leslie Brooke to be useful in drama sessions. The drawings by Brooke are so unique that using them with children is a helpful experience in aesthetics, in addition to drama.

ple, using characterization, may help. Once, while working with a group of kindergarten children, I used Grace Hallock's poem about snakes.[8]

SNAKES AND SNAILS

Through the grasses tall and slim
All about the water's rim,
Lie the slimy secret trails
Of the water-snakes and snails.

We delighted in moving through the mind-created swamp grasses as threatening snakes. However, this particular group of kindergarten children was ready to progress beyond simple movement to more complex characterizations; so, we stopped and talked about snakes. Some of the questions we considered were:

1. Are all snakes alike?
2. If not, how are they different?
3. How would a heavy, fat, old father rattler, steeped in the sun, move?
4. How might he be different from a lithe young grass snake?
5. If you were hungry, how would you move differently than if you were full of a foolish mouse dinner?

These and other questions stimulated the children to think of differences, and we were on our way to a simple understanding of characterization. Similarly, though they had worked on characterization previously, a sixth-grade class especially enjoyed further chances to develop skills of characterization. One time we used the nonsense rhyme about the old lady so silly she swallowed a whole menagerie.[9]

POOR OLD LADY

Poor old Lady, she swallowed a fly,
I don't know why she swallowed a fly.
Poor old Lady, I think she'll die.

---

[8]From the book BIRD IN THE BUSH by Grace Taber Hallock. Copyright, 1930, by E. P. Dutton & Co., Inc. Renewal © 1958 by Grace Taber Hallock. Published by E. P. Dutton & Co., Inc. and used with their permission. An interesting version can be found in *The Reading of Poetry*, by William D. Sheldon et al. (Boston: Allyn & Bacon, 1966), p. 331. This selection of poetry, with whimsical drawings by Don Madden, is prefaced by a brief but helpful section on how to approach poetry, times for using it, how to choose poems, and how they lead to self-expression.

[9]"Poor Old Lady" (author unknown), in *The Sound of Poetry*, Mary C. Austin and Queenie B. Mills (Boston: Allyn & Bacon, 1967), p. 251.

26   The "What" of Spontaneous Drama

> Poor old lady, she swallowed a spider.
> It squirmed and wriggled and turned inside her.
> She swallowed the spider to catch the fly.
> I don't know why she swallowed a fly.
> Poor old lady, I think she'll die.
>
> Poor old lady, she swallowed a bird.
> How absurd! She swallowed a bird.
> She swallowed the bird to catch the spider,
> She swallowed the spider to catch the fly,
> I don't know why she swallowed a fly.
> Poor old Lady, I think she'll die.
>
> Poor old Lady, she swallowed a cat.
> Think of that! She swallowed a cat.
> She swallowed the cat to catch the bird.
> She swallowed the bird to catch the spider,
> She swallowed the spider to catch the fly,
> I don't know why she swallowed a fly.
> Poor old lady, I think she'll die.

Ordinarily, we would consider the sixth graders too sophisticated for such a poem, but in this case it proved good stimulus for character extension. I read the poem, we laughed over it, and then we sang an impromptu version of it which the children had learned in their music class. Then we began our real work and explored verbally some questions as:

1. What is the old lady really like?
2. Was she always as silly as she is now?
3. If not, what experiences might have made her the way she is?
4. What kinds of problems could she have? How might she react to these problems?

After a discussion of her peculiarities, we divided up into pairs of small groups. One of the groups was to invent a problem for the hungry old lady, and the other small group was to create her response to the problem, thereby establishing their conception of her character. What the questioning and improvising did was to challenge the children to think more deeply about the woman, to expand and develop their characterization of her. In the story she is a two-dimensional character, seen as a silhouette set against a series of bizarre behaviors. We attempted to examine her: her characteristics, her thoughts and attitudes, her reasons for the behaviors, and her responses to problems and people. In the process, we created several different versions of the old lady and could compare and contrast these. In addition, this drama session also provided many opportunities for creating other characters who were in some way involved with the old lady and her problem.

Process Quality

Aware of the danger of unnecessarily raising the dichotomy of process versus content, it still does seem important to point out that spontaneous drama is more a process for elementary school children rather than a content area with specific grade or level expectations.

While it is true that for college-age students and teachers there is content *about* drama to be learned, the same is of less importance in the case of drama used *with* elementary school children. Drama is primarily a process used with *many* materials to evoke responses from children.

Children certainly do learn about such things as characterization, mood, plot, conflict, and rhythm, but they learn about these drama techniques with any material. For example, it does not matter whether the leader uses *Snow White* or *King Midas* to develop ideas about characterization, or *Sleeping Beauty* or *Pandora's Box* for mood development. If neither one of these interests the leader and the group, he may choose an entirely different story motivation—perhaps one seldom or never used before by a drama leader in developing ideas of characterization or mood.

Thus it is possible for children to leave an elementary school drama program with highly developed drama abilities without ever having worked with the same motivational material as other children in a different elementary school's drama program.

Drama and Language Growth

Children who have regular experiences with drama will gain in facility and expressiveness in many areas of language. An experimental study done by William E. Blank[10] points out clearly some language learnings accomplished through dramatics. Blank studied three aspects of children's development: voice qualities (including articulation and tone flexibility), personality factors, and vocabulary. Using two groups of school children, one which met weekly during the school year for creative drama and one which did not, Blank administered pre- and post-tests in the three areas of concern. The report of the research indicated that in vocabulary and in the voice qualities which he measured, Blank found that the experimental group showed a mean improvement over

---

[10]William Earl Blank, "The Effectiveness of Creative Dramatics in Developing Voice, Vocabulary and Personality", *Speech Monographs* 11 (August 1954), p. 190.

the control group with critical ratios significant at the .01 level. Creative dramatics had been effective in stimulating growth in voice quality, personality factors, and size of vocabulary. The two language factors are of most interest to us and, therefore, will be discussed further.

It seems, then, that one approach to justifying creative dramatics as an integral, rather than a peripheral, part of an elementary language arts program is the possibilities it offers for growth in knowledge about language. What particular aspects of language growth does drama encourage?

Vocabulary Growth

As Blank found experimentally—which spontaneous dramatics leaders have known intuitively for some time—one aspect of language growth which drama encourages is that of vocabulary development. Certainly, teachers must be concerned with this because of the crucial relationship between vocabulary development and success in school. By vocabulary development we do not mean, however, the learning of specific lists of words. We have ample evidence that this is not effective. The recent publication on vocabulary teaching by the National Council of Teachers of English surveys studies of such teaching and determines that new approaches must be found.[11] What we need to pursue is that passionate involvement with words, and the wonder at what they can do, which makes coming across an unknown word a challenge rather than a bore. Not nearly enough children leave elementary school caught up in the adventure of words.

The delight in words as objects to be explored, played with, and reveled in, which is manifested in young children, is seldom seen in adults. Somewhere along the way too many lose this sense of the wonder of words.

In the college methods course I teach, the textbook we use asks readers to deal with such words as lalling, denigrate, obviate, and attribution. From their conversation and results in tests and written work, it is obvious that most of these college juniors (supposedly an above average group) skip blithely over these words, extracting whatever partial kernels of meaning they can from the sentences. They are either too busy or too indifferent to succumb to the enchantment which comes from tracking down the meaning of a new word.

---

[11]Walter T. Petty et al., *The State of Knowledge About the Teaching of Vocabulary* (Champaign: National Council of Teachers of English, 1968). The book examines current procedures for teaching vocabulary and then presents and analyzes eleven recent studies. There is a chapter on the linguistic considerations related to vocabulary study. The summary and recommendations should be of interest to a teacher interested in improving his techniques in this area.

What is your curiosity quotient about words? Take these examples:

Have you ever felt rubicund?
Have you ever seen dihiscence?
Have you ever had a papeterie?

How many of them do you know? Do they intrigue you enough that you would like to know more about them?

How are we to get this involvement with words so we develop adults whose curiosity is piqued by unfamiliar ones? Certainly not, as mentioned earlier, by drilling children on lists. But spontaneous dramatics can provide one way. Much of the literature used as motivation for spontaneous drama will result in exposure to new and unfamiliar words. Ward says that in using literature to stimulate dramatics, "... the children will take hold of as much of the original language as they are able for the sound of it is fascinating to them."[12]

Davis has a similar approach which he calls *impressional treatment*. This approach:

> ... gives the child a feeling or an attitude toward material or planned experiences. The child can be said to be initiated into certain activities or ideas. This feeling is derived from empathic methods ... a great many of the experiences provided ... should be given impressional treatment.[13]

Davis further explains that "the child is exposed to the material ... but no major effort is made to define or fix the feeling or ... experience."

In using drama to further vocabulary growth, the leader is not after specific words to be memorized, but rather a captivating exposure to enough words to sensitize children to their "lure and lore." Several excellent examples of this are contained in the book entitled *Push Back the Desks*, written by an experienced elementary school teacher, Albert Cullum. In the first of these he describes how he worked with a group of kindergarten children. Cullum writes as follows:

> From my meager linen closet I sacrificed a good white sheet to make a dramatic entrance into the kindergarten ... As a roaming language arts teacher I was able to indulge in such activity ...

---

[12]Winifred Ward, *Playmaking with Children* (New York: Appleton-Century-Crofts, 1957), p. 187.

[13]David C. Davis, *Patterns of Primary Education* (New York: Harper & Row, 1963), p. 41. Though an older book now out of print, this one by Davis (probably available in libraries) has much to say of interest to the primary teacher. Davis' presentation of impressional, foundational, and skill treatment of subject matter is particularly unusual.

30 *The "What" of Spontaneous Drama*

> There I was in the middle of the kindergarten covered with my last good sheet, in which two holes had been cut out for my eyes. I saw twenty-two pairs of eyes looking at me. "I am a friendly apparition," I slowly stated. "What's that?" asked five-year-old Tony. They all started to talk at once, of course, so I asked them to sit in a circle, and I sat in the center. I proceeded to whirl about in a flashing dervish manner and explained to them that for Halloween I was going to be a very friendly apparition. "What do I look like?" Finally Anette guessed that I was dressed as a ghost. They then took turns wearing the large sheet and ... flew through the kindergarten air as friendly apparitions. It was simple for them to accept apparition as a good kindergarten word.[14]

Certainly this is simple dramatization—the very beginning steps—but even at this stage the children take delight in responding to words.

Cullum also describes his work with other children, and in the following section, writes of using Shakespeare as motivation:

> It is so simple for a third-grade teacher to introduce *Julius Caesar* by letting his children pretend to be the fickle, violent crowd ... no one is daydreaming when Juliet Capulet hesitates to drink the liquid that will make her appear dead; no one is looking at the clock when the two very young royal princes are ushered into the Tower of London to their death.
>
> Shakespeare may be for scholars to debate and discuss ... but he is also for Corky, a fifth-grader who died beautifully as Julius Caesar. There are "murderers" galore in the elementary school ready to help Macbeth kill Banquo; many a fifth- and sixth-grade girl can readily whip up a moment of insanity as Ophelia.[15]

It is one thing to let children respond with fervor to words (and it does build a sensitivity to them), but do these words remain with a child? Cullum feels that they do and describes the results he achieved in using this means of increasing language growth with his group of kindergarten children:

> It was exciting to see them go home during the school year as twenty-two eerie apparitions ... well-trained pachyderms ... [or] proud, snorting stallions ... They carried their big words home to astounded

---

[14]Albert Cullum, *Push Back the Desks* (New York: Citation Press, 1967), pp. 60–61. In this unique account of his work with children, Cullum tells how he fostered creativity in his children using his own creative ability in many subject areas. The book is easy to read and highly recommended for the myriad of ideas which can be gleaned from it.

[15]Ibid., p. 82.

parents, grandparents, and older brothers and sisters. They were proud of their new words. Together we had added sixty new words to their speaking vocabulary. At the end of the year I devised a test to see how well they had retained their big words. Without any review, over ninety percent of the class scored one hundred. The words were still alive.[16]

In summary, what the spontaneous drama leader accomplishes is to share words with children. As Lewis says so well, " . . . the pupils are off their guard . . . and it is then that something is not learned, but absorbed through the intuitive channel."[17]

In addition to this unconscious assimilation of words, there are some vocabulary words which become part of a child's speaking vocabulary because they are closely related to creative drama. One example, which Crist uses,[18] is the term *sincerity*—an honest response to the motivation—which other leaders refer to as "staying in character." Leaders regularly use such terms as *environment* and *symbol,* even with young children.

Paralanguage

Another area of children's growth in language through dramatics is that of paralanguage—pitch, stress, and juncture. Leaders work to help children to understand pitch, the high or low sound; stress, the accent in a word; and juncture, the stops or pauses between words. Children grow to a *conscious* knowledge of how they can use this expressive overlay on language. Probably all children, except those with severe emotional and/or learning problems, *unconsciously* assimilate the basic features of paralanguage along with other early language learning, which experts unanimously tell us takes place largely before the age of six. Most children come to school, undoubtedly, as fully in control of paralanguage as they are in the more basic verbal symbols of language. Beyond their basic mastery, however, the school provides children with scant opportunity for conscious study and learning about manipulating these three elements to convey ideas more expressively.

Why should children learn something of these features of our language? Linguists and other language students agree that they are

---

[16]Ibid., p. 65.

[17]C. Day Lewis, "The Poem and the Lesson" *English Journal* 55 (March 1968), pp. 321–327.

[18]Rita Crist, *All That I Am.* Sixteen twenty-minute videotapes on creative dramatics, they are available on lease from the Great Plains National Instructional Television Library, Lincoln, Nebraska.

critical factors in communication. For instance, psychologists Mehrabian and Ferris[19] have estimated that of the total impact of the message, 7 percent is accomplished by basic verbal symbols, while 38 percent is conveyed by vocal overlays of pitch, stress, and juncture—paralanguage. In addition, they estimate that 55 percent of the message is determined by the accompanying facial expressions called *kinesics*, which we will consider later. Apparently, only a small portion of the message is transmitted by the basic verbal symbols.

If these extra-verbal factors are this crucial in communication, then it is apparent children should learn about them, so that they can grow to be more effective in using their language.

Examination of basic language textbooks reveals that little is done to make children aware of how they can achieve desired effects by manipulating pitch, stress, and juncture. While much work is included about the correct use of went and gone and see and saw, little is concerned with helping children to experiment with these three elements of paralanguage to become more effective speakers of English. There are, happily, a few interesting exceptions among the more recent texts.[20]

What we are concerned with here is the conscious control of paralanguage, in order to create desired effects. By motivating the child to improvise dialogue for a variety of characters, dramatics helps to raise to a conscious level the idea that different people speak in different ways, making resulting effects different.

Sometimes these learnings come up incidentally as they are related to story motivation. It is possible to have excellent sessions experimenting with voices necessary to a particular story. In using the *Three Billy Goats Gruff* with young children, for example, a leader may explore such questions as:

1. What does a troll sound like?
2. Do all trolls sound the same? Does a river troll (as the one in the story is described) sound the same as a forest troll? Would a cave troll sound different?
3. How does a father troll sound when he is content after a filling dinner of succulent goat?
4. How does a mother troll sound when she is nagging her lethargic husband to get a tender goat for dinner?

---

[19]Albert Mehrabian and Susan R. Ferris, "Inference of Attitudes from Non-Verbal Communication in Two Channels," *Journal of Consulting Psychology* 31, no. 3 (June 1967), pp. 248–252.

[20]See for example: Muriel Crosby, *The World of Language* (Chicago: Follett Educational Corporation, 1970), Book 6, pp. 152–156, 187–189, and Book 5, pp. 22–31; Harry W. Sartain et al., *English Is Our Language* (Boston: D. C. Heath & Co., 1968), Book 6, pp. 48–49, and Book 5, pp. 50–52, 104–105.

Children find such questions as these delightful. They provide an opportunity to create story line (plot) spontaneously, but more importantly, such questions allow children to explore paralanguage, to play with and speculate upon the speech of this created troll family, and to see how imaginative they can be in creating the trolls with their own voices.

At other times, we stimulate these learnings purposely, as when we confront children with pictures of people and ask them to create voices and manipulate pitch, stress, and juncture to make the character come alive. Confronted with a picture with only visual clues, the child is challenged to create a person using the three elements of paralanguage to augment the basic verbal symbols.

Sometimes we work with just a sentence in isolation to explore the variety of effects which are possible in a minimal combination of words. Given a sentence used by one of the characters in an improvisation, children enjoy experimenting to see what different connotations can be expressed by altering the stress on words. Sixth graders enjoy working with such sentences as: "My, that's a pretty green dress you have on today." There is a myriad of interpretations possible:

1. My, that's a *pretty* green dress you have on today. (Interpretation: You sure wore a homely green one yesterday.)
2. My, *that's* a pretty green dress you have on today. (Interpretation: I like that one, but the one on the rack leaves me cold.)
3. My, that's a *pretty green* dress you have on today. (Interpretation: If it were any more green I don't think I could stand it!)
4. My, that's a pretty green *dress* you have on today. (Interpretation: But, you're wearing an ugly fuchsia hat.)
5. My, that's a pretty green dress *you* have on today. (Interpretation: The girl beside you is wearing an outlandish turquoise dress.)
6. My, that's a pretty green dress you have on *today*. (Interpretation: So, at last, you've worn a pretty dress.)

Sometimes, spontaneous drama leaders work with more abstract sounds than the recognizable words and paralanguage we have been discussing. Recently, I had the opportunity to watch Miss Ann Flagg, an experienced dramatics leader with the Evanston schools,[21] explore the abstract sounds made by the Furies Pandora released from the box. Improvising

---

[21]Evanston, Illinois, public schools have the oldest and most complete dramatics program for elementary school children in the country. Directed by the ebullient Mrs. Anne Thurman and staffed with over a dozen drama leaders, the schools provide a continuous program of sequentially organized drama classes well worth making the effort to see. The school district welcomes visitors interested in drama.

on the basic idea, fourth-, fifth-, and sixth-grade children decided that threatening movement was not enough, so they explored such questions as:

1. Would each of the Furies make the same sound?
2. How could the sounds differ? In pitch? In constancy? In duration?
3. What sound would Hope make while trying to get out of the box? After it was released by Pandora?
4. How would the sounds made by the Furies change when they heard the sounds made by Hope?

The children worked with this idea and changed volumes, breaks durations, inflections, and other elements to create a composition of abstract verbal sound, devoid of recognizable English words, but nonetheless conveying the conflict between the Furies and Hope. It was an exciting experience: children, stimulated by contact with a literary form and encouraged to create using a basic idea, were learning how expressive their voices could be, even apart from conventional verbal symbols. Rather sophisticated learnings for an elementary school!

In these examples, we have seen how children can learn consciously some ideas about paralanguage which were previously known unconsciously. These are ideas which remain unconscious in far too many adults. Who has not had the experience of hearing someone say "Good morning" when the real message conveyed by paralanguage was "All this is too much bother, and you're the cause of it!" We use paralanguage as adults each day and, if we can teach children how to manipulate the three elements consciously, we shall be teaching them how to use one of the most expressive devices of a marvelously flexible language as they increase their ability to communicate.

Kinesics

Another aspect of language about which children can learn in spontaneous dramatics is kinesics. Lefevre defines the term to include:

> ... all bodily gestures, nudges, nods, finger, hand and arm signals, shrugs, and facial gestures such as winks, smiles, sneers and leers—the whole gamut of expressive actions, so important in ... interpretation and in the small events of daily life.[22]

---

[22]Carl A. Lefevre, *Linguistics, English and the Language Arts* (Boston: Allyn & Bacon, 1970), pp. 174–175.

You will remember that Mahrabian and Ferris, as mentioned earlier, estimate that this aspect of language may account for up to 55 percent of the meaning of the message.

Despite this, and the universal use we make of this aspect of language, an examination of elementary language materials reveals that, like paralanguage, kinesics is seldom a matter of much concern to the authors of language series. Dramatics can make up for this lack, as children examine characters in depth and work to convey their understandings through the use of extra-linguistic features.

A group of fourth- and fifth-grade children recently worked with the old folk tale entitled "The Stone in the Road"[23] and concentrated especially on the reaction of the villagers to finding the stone in the otherwise meticulously maintained kingdom. Their leader talked with them about nonverbal means they could use to develop characterizations of the villagers, as in this session each child chose to be one of the villagers. The differences in the shrugs, hand and arm movements, frowns and gestures, and other kinesics used made obvious to an observer the character of the soldier, scholar, carpenter, and other inhabitants. In the evaluation session following the improvisation, the children enjoyed comparing the way one child's characterization differed from that of another's. As they did this, the children evaluated which kinesics conveyed ideas they wanted to communicate, which needed to be modified to be more effective, and which they needed more practice in using.

Harold Allen[24] recommends doing a conscious study of kinesics and spatial relationships at the high school level. Spontaneous drama leaders, however, can begin developing an understanding and appreciation of these communication factors long before children reach high school.

Spontaneous Oral Composition

An even more encompassing goal than the specific ones mentioned earlier is that of encouraging growth in the child's ability in spontaneous oral composition, i.e., impromptu or extemporaneous invention. We work for this goal when as drama leaders we work with plot development. Ward says that giving children experiences in "thinking on their feet" and expressing ideas fearlessly is an important concern of creative dramatics. She further notes:

---

[23] The story is included in Schiller et al., *Language and How to Use It* (Chicago: Scott, Foresman & Co., 1969), Book 4, p. 148.

[24] Harold B. Allen, "Porro Unum Est Necessarium," in *The Hues of English* (Champaign: National Council of Teachers of English, 1969), pp. 91–109.

When older children are asked what ... [drama] is worth to them besides being so enjoyable, they often think first of this objective because they feel so strongly the need both for the poise which comes from being articulate and the power it gives them among their fellows.[25]

One of the ways Ward suggests for getting at this ability is to allow a child to give a lead sentence, e.g., "The boy was uncertain about what to do now." Without allowing the child who contributed the sentence to explain it, she selects volunteers who want to build an impromptu scene around the lead sentence.[26]

Another successful way to stimulate oral composition is to take a standard piece of literature and present an additional problem related to it. For example:

1. What would have happened if the goat couldn't get across the bridge?
2. How else could Midas have solved his problem?
3. What would have happened if the slipper had fit Cinderella's sister?
4. Who could have come to the aid of the gingerbread boy as he rode across the river on the fox's back?
5. Who else besides the knave might have stolen the Queen's tarts? Why?

Children respond easily to this type of problem and develop an oral proficiency in the process.

Recently, I used this approach with a group of third-grade children; the motivation was the Mother Hubbard rhyme which Torrance[27] uses as one of his tests of creativity. The rhyme, as you remember, reads:

> Old Mother Hubbard went to her cupboard,
> to get her poor dog a bone.
> When she got there, the cupboard was bare,
> and so the poor dog had none.

The question posed to the children was, "Instead of simply letting the poor dog go hungry, what *else* might Old Mother Hubbard have

---

[25]Ward, *Playmaking with Children*, op. cit., p. 8.

[26]This idea, the use of starter sentences (also called *conflict lines*) is explained further on p. 87 of Chapter 4.

[27]E. Paul Torrance, *Guiding Creative Talent* (Englewood Cliffs, N. J.: Prentice-Hall, 1962), pp. 245–246.

done?" Among the more inventive responses suggested, which lent themselves to playing in spontaneous dramatics, were these:

1. She went to the butcher and asked for a job. He was in need of help, so he hired her to cut meat from the bones. At the end of the day, she got to keep the bones.
2. She went to the police station and got their help in tracking down the thief who had stolen all the bones.
3. She planted a garden in which she grew many vegetables. The extra ones she sold at a stand and used the money to buy bones for her dog.
4. She went out begging from door to door, asking for a penny at each house. The townspeople were embarrassed to give her just a penny, so they gave her more. When she was done collecting, she had so much money she built a mansion and bought all the bones she wanted.
5. Since she didn't have bones, she made up some porridge, and it was so good the dog ate that instead.[28]

Sometimes, instead of presenting a problem to children, we simply describe two people in a situation and let children create both story line and dialogue. The results are not always predictable. Children learn through their improvisation, but it may be an other than pleasant revelation of perceptions for the teacher to listen to two third graders improvising, one as a mother or father, the other as a child. I recently worked with a group of third graders who used words, paralanguage, kinesics, and movement to create a story line about adults and children. All of the improvisations were disturbing; despite the fact that the stimulus had been neutral, all of the adults were cast in repressive, controlling roles. However, the exercise proved to be good for the children, as it provided a way to play out their feelings of powerlessness in a socially acceptable mode. Such an experience does give one pause to think about the relations between adults and children.

It was similarly interesting to listen to a group of college juniors as they paired off to create spontaneous dialogue between a principal and a teacher. Their use of the elements of communication was creative, but the hidden attitudes revealed towards principals as authority figures would chill the heart of the most determined public school dictator.

---

[28]If you want to use this motivation, the pictures in *Old Mother Hubbard and Her Dog* (New York: Whittlesey House, 1960) illustrated by Paul Galdone are a delight to share. The pictures include the slightly addled old woman who makes constant forays searching for presents for her talented, though slightly disheveled, dog.

Children *can* learn to become proficient in spontaneous oral composition, though this is a skill which is slow to develop and difficult to measure. Does this growing oral ability affect a child's written expression? Does the oral facility gained mirror corresponding growth in written composition? A tantalizing question—waiting for an interested researcher!

Some Other Uses for Dramatics

Now that we have considered at some length the specific language uses of spontaneous drama, we will consider briefly other uses of drama, because dramatics is not limited to the language program.[29] The perceptive teacher is able to see many subject areas in which to use dramatics. One inventive leader interested in social studies helped intermediate children to better understand themselves by working with the idea of fear interpreting an explorer's feelings as he set foot on the white-grained edge of an unfamiliar continent. Another helped children evolve some sensitive rhythmic patterns based on the concept of number bases in mathematics. His group, divided into different bases, interwove, moved, split, and regrouped and then enjoyed working with the concept on paper after they had interpreted it rhythmically.

Still a third leader helped kindergarten children in a simple fashion to respond to the ebullience of a Sousa march and later led sixth graders to a sensitive response to the brooding and evocative counter rhythm in Ravel's *Bolero.*

In science a second-grade leader used the life cycle of flowering plants to explore the possibilities of dramatic improvisation. He enriched the topic considerably by helping the children to understand the subtle differences between larkspur and hollyhock, fuchsia and dandelion, and how to interpret what these flowers' responses might be to outside influences. The hollyhock and the larkspur responded to the effect of the wind, for example, and the children understood and played the differing effects of the sun on the shade-loving fuchsia and the sun-loving dandelion.

Other drama leaders have found opportunities to incorporate drama into the school program in other areas, but these should suffice to make the point. While there are many applications of this art in the curriculum, the ones we are most concerned with here are those integral to the language arts program. Readers interested in other uses for dra-

---

[29]Hoetker, *Dramatics and the Teaching of Literature,* op. cit., pp. 31–32. The author includes an extensive bibliography of periodical articles describing both subject matter applications of drama and its use with exceptional children.

matics will find the articles which have been written on them of help in explaining the wide scope of drama in the elementary school (see Chapter 6).

Summary

In this chapter I have attempted to do two things:

1. To detail the diverse activities included in spontaneous drama so that you may have a clearer idea of the nature of the activities this book is encouraging you to engage in.
2. To identify the many types of language growth which may take place as a result of your using drama as an aspect of your language arts program.

The problem which remains now is a procedural one; given a group of thirty children, how do *you*—a teacher in a self-contained classroom of average size—"do" drama? Perhaps you aren't lucky enough to work in a school system which employs specially trained drama leaders, but that doesn't mean your children can't have the benefits of regular drama experiences. If you are convinced of the values of drama, the next chapter should help you to learn some ways in which you can lead spontaneous drama sessions with your children.

3

The "How" of Spontaneous Drama

To separate the "what" of a complex subject from the "how" of that subject is often a futile and frustrating task. One reason for attempting to do so is to point out clearly some of the factors which influence the success one expects to have. To that end I have attempted in this chapter to present some ideas related to how one "does" spontaneous drama with children.

Characteristics of the Leader

One of the most crucial factors in drama is the leader. What are the requirements of a successful leader? Are teachers likely to be good drama leaders, or should children work with someone especially trained in improvisation techniques?

Efforts to characterize the "typical" elementary school teacher usually fail, simply because of the diversity of people who are, for a myriad of reasons, drawn into teaching. Similarly, I have come to the conclusion after talking with many different drama leaders that to characterize the spontaneous dramatics leader is a difficult task.

Are we then to assume, confronted with the array of personalities who work with children, that *anyone* is likely to be successful with drama? I think not—though I have no grounds other than subjective ones for this contention. Teachers who have tried dramatics with their children and failed are not likely to talk about it.

What kinds of people are likely to succeed as dramatics leaders? Several other authors have given their opinions on this question, and someone thinking about launching a program would do well to read these (see references Chapter 6). For the purposes of this chapter, I will discuss four characteristics which I feel are basic to a successful drama leader. These characteristics are certainly nothing new—wishfully, all classroom teachers possess them—but they are especially important to the teacher when he is serving as a spontaneous dramatics leader.

Flexibility

The willingness to abandon a previous plan in the event something more interesting or more worthwhile comes up during a session is an important trait of the drama leader. An actual example may serve to demonstrate why this is important.

While visiting a student teacher recently, I watched a group of second graders improvising on some written motivation about Christmas. The leader had created some situations, one of which involved a young sister who was sick on Christmas Eve. The children working with this idea attacked their challenge with dispatch, but this resulted in some rather poor playing. The sister was unceremoniously picked up and lugged laboriously down the imagined stairs much as one might carry a heavy sack of salt for a water softener. No attempt was made either to pick up the invalid gently or to deposit her carefully on the davenport once she was moved to the living room.

Basically, the idea was a potentially profitable one, but it failed—primarily because the student teacher was more interested in "acting-out" than in a valid improvisation. To make the lesson a success he would have had to abandon his plans to hurry along to three other improvisations and, instead, turn the group's attention to such questions as:

1. How do we carry someone?
2. Are there any special things we do to carry someone who is sick?
3. How heavy was the sister?
4. How could we pick her up in order not to make her sicker?
5. How would we arrange her on the davenport once we had carried her to it?

This does, of course, change the whole thrust of the lesson, from one of improvising superficially on several ideas created previously by the teacher to one of more spontaneous and yet more thoughtful response to questions evolved at the time. Such a change in thrust is admittedly difficult to effect, especially when the leader is new and inexperienced; this is probably because, to effect such profitable changes, one must be listening intently and continuously for ideas from the children throughout the entire lesson.

Another student teacher, with less singleness of purpose, noted that children, in trimming a tree, were simply picking an endless succession of imaginary ornaments out of one hand and with the other putting them on branches. He saw the children never needed to:

1. put hangers on the ornaments.
2. go to a box or other source for more ornaments.
3. unwrap the ornaments.
4. move a branch to find room for an ornament.

This was a discrepancy in the improvisation; despite the fact that he, too, had other groups which had not yet taken part, the student teacher took time to talk with his students. He discussed with them all the components of the act of hanging an ornament on a tree, and they practiced these components together. Then the children were ready to do their improvisation again, and there was a noticeable improvement in believability.

Another illustration may reinforce the need to be aware of cues from the children which can lead to more genuinely helpful spontaneous creation. In a third-grade classroom the children were presenting their ideas about Christmas Eve, which involved children sleeping. One of the boys in the "audience" indicated his urge to participate by asking: "Why are they all doing it (sleeping) exactly alike?" Again the leader was presented with an opportunity, from a child in the group, to do some helpful work in considering individualization of improvisation.[1] Because he was inexperienced, this particular leader missed the child's comment and did not capitalize on the possibilities inherent in his remark.

Ability to Listen

This leads to the second characteristic—the drama leader's immense *ability to listen*. As teachers, many of us expect children to listen to us but, frequently, the reciprocal nature of this act is ignored. We expound; children listen. Indeed, several studies have indicated that this is what children in elementary schools do most frequently throughout the school day.[2] In dramatics sessions, however, the teacher must listen as

---

[1] This idea, also called particularization of individual movements, gestures, or behaviors, is further explained on p. 91 of Chapter 4.

[2] The studies most frequently cited are those by Rankin and Wilt, both of which are summarized in Paul C. Burns et al., *Language Arts in Childhood Education* (Chicago: Rand McNally, 1971), pp. 84–85.

intently as he hopes the children do. Without this listening, he will never hear the many comments, often fragmentary or not directed specifically to him, which can result in a much richer experience for the children.

This does not mean, of course, that he changes plans willy-nilly, just following comments with each change of the wind. This type of program would not help children to learn in each of the areas of spontaneous dramatics. There are times when he does hear a comment of the nature described and simply makes a mental note of it—a referent to return to later. Perhaps because of the involvement level of the children, the closeness to reaching the desired goal for the day, or the unrelatedness of the comment, the leader decides to ignore a perfectly valid comment. This is a sophisticated sifting of possibilities, the continual reordering of priorities which a drama leader does during a session. When such an ability is developed, the session can take on a flexibility leading to some valid learning experiences for children; without such ability, the sessions may develop into the rather wooden "playlets" which are so often confused with dramatics. The remedy: concentrate on the ability to listen.

This ability to listen is related to the flexibility mentioned earlier, but which may be a flexibility difficult to develop. We have some information of an experimental nature which indicates that many people drawn to teaching are conforming, rule-following, and noninnovative.[3]

Teacher education programs appear to draw a large proportion of conforming individuals, people who would be too inhibited to get down on the floor with a group of children and be a snake right along with them. Unfortunately, it appears that even the student-teaching experience—which is to be a time of experimenting—often results in an increase of conforming behaviors.[4]

Finally, even teaching in the public schools tends to limit the creativity of too many teachers; they succumb to the pressures of principals to prepare and turn in lesson plans and of other teachers' grade-level expectations.

---

[3]For example see Phillip W. Jackson, *Life in Classrooms* (New York: Holt, Rinehart & Winston, 1968). The author describes with uncanny accuracy the results of his extensive research into the everyday "business" of an elementary classroom. He views what he sees with a fresh eye, reports compassionately but with vigor, and causes us to reexamine procedures we have taken for granted.

[4]Laurence J. Iannaccone, "Student Teaching: A Transitional Stage in the Making of a Teacher," *Theory Into Practice*, Vol. I–II (April 1963), pp. 73–80. The researcher discovered that the student teachers' value position changed almost completely during the semester, and allowed them at the end to accept and rationalize many teacher-centered, directive behaviors which before had been abhorrent to them.

This problem is well presented by Clements[5] in a beguiling book in which he discusses in a fey, though serious, manner the constraints, both real and imaginary, with which the teacher is encompassed. Thus, being flexible enough to do dramatics with children is a characteristic not all teachers possess. If the teacher did possess this characteristic, it may have been suppressed, either during student teaching or full-time teaching. The encouraging thing, however, is that it is a characteristic which can be developed if the teacher is interested.

Ability to Ask Stimulating Questions

Another characteristic, related to flexibility, is the *ability to ask stimulating questions.* Why should the dramatics leader need to be a questioner? Throughout the sample materials in Chapter 5, and in other sections of the book, you will see the emphasis on the teacher's need to be a skilled question asker. To ask the right kind of questions will be difficult for *many* teachers. Research on the types of questions teachers ask is not encouraging.[6] This is true even among art teachers, hopefully one of the most creative groups of people at work with children in the elementary school. The results of a study done by Clements reported stimulating, open-ended questions to be at a minimum. Apparently, art teachers also find it difficult to ask this type of question.[7]

Because the art of questioning is difficult to develop, the teacher will probably need to practice asking questions and will need to ask many, many questions before his skill is well developed. Not such closed questions as:

1. Who is Billy's friend?
2. What happened when father came home from work?
3. Why couldn't Betty find the answer to her problem?

But such provocative, stimulating questions as:

1. What other things could the bears who had no porridge do?

---

[5]H. Millard Clements et al., *Social Study: Inquiry in Elementary Classrooms* (Indianapolis: Bobbs-Merrill, 1966). Though it deals with social studies and is, thus, not directly germane to this discussion of drama, the book is well written, and I recommend it highly to teachers interested in an innovative social studies program. It is a fascinating methods book—an unusual thing!

[6]A summary of several research projects related to this question, and some helpful material designed to improve teachers' question-asking ability is included in George D. and Evelyn B. Spache, *Reading in the Elementary School* (Boston: Allyn & Bacon, 1969), pp. 481–491.

[7]Robert D. Clements, "Art Teachers Classroom Questioning," *Art Education* 18 (April 1965), pp. 16–19.

2. What would have happened if Cinderella's foot hadn't fit the glass slipper?
3. What would have happened if Little Red Riding Hood had gotten lost in the forest, and never arrived at Grandmother's house?

One of the ways to learn the art of questioning is to listen carefully to children—their art of asking questions is enviable, especially when they are young. A third-grade child, part of a reading group studying *Midas Touch*, thoughtfully asked how Midas could still move around after the touch was bestowed: "Wouldn't his clothes turn to gold because they touched his body?" The teacher, inept at handling such intelligent and provocative questions, and also probably because the teacher's manual provided no answer, ignored his unique question.

Certainly, this was a point at which to stop the lesson and encourage the children to discuss their ideas about the child's question. The teacher could have let the children explore this idea, which was an unusual one. He might have suggested they compare several versions of the story to see if other versions offered any clues. Further, he might have discussed with them the similarity between the Achille's Heel myth[8] (an example of a localized physical quality) and the Midas Touch myth. Listen to the types of questions your children ask—then try asking similarly exciting ones.

You will be mostly on your own in practicing the art of questioning, for there is little encouragement in most school materials to raise the level of questions to ask. Questions in basal reading materials, for example, are too frequently banal and literal; other subject areas do little better. There are, however, some books devoted solely to the art of asking questions, and the inexpensive paperback by Sanders is a very helpful one.[9] It would certainly be beneficial to get a copy of this and read it.

Another suggestion, related more specifically to questions in dramatics, might be of help. Take a poem you enjoy from one of the poetry anthologies. (It is probably simpler to begin this practice using a poem because of its shorter length). Attempt to ask some motivational questions concerning it. Ask some questions related to the images which are

---

[8]This myth is included with many others in *Bulfinch's Mythology,* illustrated by Elinore Blaisdell (New York: Thomas Y. Crowell Co., n.d.) An excellent source of the myths, the leader will want to make his own decision regarding the illustrations. They are very effectively done in monochromatic color and are of interest because of the costume detail included. However because of the partial nudity involved, they may not be useable with all groups of children.

[9]Norris M. Sanders, *Classroom Questions: What Kinds?* (Harper & Row, 1966).

contained within the poem, and then ask some which are only suggested by, or related to, what is included in the poem. After you have created a group of questions, attempt to analyze them. Ask yourself:

1. Do they go beyond the literal level?
2. Do they capitalize on the material which is included?
3. Are they open-ended, so that children can do more than one thing in responding to them?
4. Might the questions stimulate children to ask more questions themselves?
5. Do they utilize "cues" contained in the poem which are not expanded upon by the poet?

To illustrate this procedure, I took the poem which is included below and wrote some questions which could be used to motivate children in dramatics. As you read the poem, think about what kinds of questions *you* might ask children about it.

WIND WEATHER[10]

The wind's an old woman in front of the rain
Picking up papers and laying them again;
Muttering, fussing, and slamming a door
That only comes back to be slammed at some more.

The wind's an old woman indignantly trying
To gather her goods from the rain's hasty prying.
She frightens the trees till they circle and flail.
But the sensible cows turn their back to her wail.
Yet, when the rain starts its imperative fall
The old-woman-wind doesn't mind it at all.
She chuckles and puffs, unconcerned as you please
At the terrible scare she has given the trees.

Below are some questions about this poem. Can you come up with some others—some better ones—based on the poem?

1. For what reasons does the poet compare the wind to an old woman? What things might be similar in their actions?

---

[10]Virginia Brasier, *Sunset Magazine* 87 (October 1941), p. 4. This poem also included in Huber, *Story and Verse for Children*, op. cit., p. 120.

2. How do people react to being in the wind before a rain? Does your reaction depend upon your age? What are you doing? What else might affect your reaction?
3. The poem mentions "gathering goods" before a rain. What might that mean? How have you prepared before a rain? How might other people prepare? Could you show us?
4. What kinds of motions might trees in the wind make? Would it depend on what kind of tree? Type and age? How might this be different at different seasons of the year?

One further word about questioning is necessary. After you have asked questions which will admit different answers and which will allow for different bodily movements in response, you must be careful to treat these answers and responses in an open-ended fashion. Even skilled drama leaders must avoid the tendency, so fatal to a vigorous discussion, to accept the first or best idea offered, thereby losing—by the failure to probe further—other ideas of potential interest. It is only by the skillful reasking of the basic question, or by the framing of related questions, that one can hope to derive the widest possible range of responses.

There is one other characteristic, or quality, of the leader of spontaneous dramatics which is very important. Indeed, perhaps it is the *most* important attribute. Do you *believe* in the values of dramatics?

The Importance of Believing

The teacher is confronted daily with requirements to teach something —by the school board, by state laws, by the principal, by interested pressure groups. Frequently, these are subjects in which he is uninterested, areas in which he is incompetent, or topics by which he is bored. Fortunately, no such pressures exist to include spontaneous dramatics as one aspect of the language arts, and the teacher is free to omit this from the program. A bit of sage advice would be for him to do so unless, and *only* unless, he completely believes in this art form as a valid means of learning. Perhaps no other instructional area in the curriculum can be as ineffective or can "fall apart" as quickly as when a teacher tries to do creative dramatics with children when he is not completely committed to it as a beneficial part of the program.

The teacher must have a conviction about the importance of helping children to learn about themselves, others, and their world through dramatics before attempting to use this art form with children. Certainly, the language arts program will continue, and no one will fault the less adventuresome teacher for *not* doing spontaneous drama with his children. If he does not truly believe in spontaneous dramatics, no quantity of glossy professional gimmicks will cover up this basic attitude, and once children discover that a leader's attitude towards spontaneous drama is not sincere, their attitudes will be affected, for children sense attitudes easily. However, if the leader *does* have a belief in spontaneous dramatics, almost any amount of technical ineptness in selecting, motivating, and questioning can be overcome.

Therefore, before attempting to do dramatics with children, the potential leader must first analyze his own attitudes toward the art. The following questions may help.

1. Do I really believe children can learn as much from themselves and from other children as from books?
2. Do I really believe art forms are important to children? Am I willing to allocate a chunk of "prime time" during a crowded school day to these art forms?
3. Do I really believe art forms children create have intrinsic validity, or do I feel that a child's more important role in the arts is as a consumer?
4. Am I willing to take an idea and work with it, capitalizing on the contributions of children and following where the lesson leads? Or do I have to have an end in mind (and reach it) for each lesson?
5. Do I believe that all learning can be measured, and therefore will be unhappy if I cannot objectively determine *what kind* and *how much* learning has taken place?
6. Can I tolerate a rather unseemly amount of chaos (as is bound to exist for the first few sessions) in order to reach my goals of student participation and responsiveness?
7. Am I comfortable enough with myself so that I can participate with children until time to withdraw without fear of feeling foolish? Could I improvise the hop of the old father frog if the children need my participation as demonstration of my belief? How much will my dignity suffer if I do this—is my dignity more important to me than my children?
8. Can I express myself articulately enough about what I believe to be able to "sell" my ideas to parents, co-workers, and administrative superiors?

We will discuss evaluation of the dramatics session later in this chapter. For now, the potential leader is faced with different kinds of evaluation, of his own unarticulated thoughts, beliefs, and desires related to this area of the curriculum.

This emphasis on the importance of belief in drama is not intended to minimize the need for the drama leader to study and read and to work with children and then reflect, in order to learn about and refine specific skills necessary to an effective leader. It is simply important to reinforce the idea that belief in, or commitment to, the goals of drama form a major factor in the ultimate success of the drama leader.

Selecting Materials

Once the teacher has decided he is interested in trying improvised drama with his children, the immediate problem to be solved is that of materials to use. A key to success in spontaneous drama is to make sure both the materials and the motivation provide for active participation, and not simply passive discussion. In view of the previous emphasis on questions and discussion, it seems appropriate to point out that the purpose of the material—the goal towards which it is leading—is to get children involved in *doing* something. Each motivation must lend itself to this. If it does not, it is *probably* not good material for drama.

While it is perhaps true that any material *can* be used to motivate drama (if the leader is adept enough in adapting and using it), it is also true that, generally, it will be easier to make use of material that is not *simply* descriptive. The following poem, while a wonderfully evocative piece which should be read beautifully by a choral speaking choir, is of less usefulness in motivating dramatic experiences than something with more active images.

APRIL RAIN SONG[11]

Let the rain kiss you.
Let the rain beat upon your head with silver
 liquid drops.
Let the rain sing you a lullaby.

The rain makes still pools on the sidewalk.
The rain makes running pools in the gutter.
The rain plays a little sleep-song on our roof
 at night

And I love the rain.

---

[11]Langston, Hughes, *The Dream Keeper* (New York: Alfred A. Knopf, 1932). The poem is included in Isabel J. Peterson, *The First Book of Poetry* (New York: Franklin Watts, 1954), p. 87. Though it contains rather undistinguished illustrations, the book does include some fine poems for dramatics. You will find useful the poems by Milne, Meigs, and Wynne in motivating children. Other descriptive poems are also included in this useful collection.

If a teacher wanted to use the poem for its language qualities, he would need to work with children to develop ideas *suggested by* the poem, but not included there, in order to build a session based on the material. Using the film "Rainshower"[12] in conjunction with this would help establish the mood. The teacher's skill in questioning would need to be used, however, to make this material of utmost usefulness in a dramatic session. The poem does provide "cues" for further questioning which could be developed by the teacher if he is perceptive. The following questions expand upon these cues:

1. What things could you do in one of the still pools on the sidewalk? How do you get around a wide, but shallow, pool? What happens when you walk out of a shallow pool? How could you splash through one of these pools? What would happen if there was a hole in one of your rubbers when you walked through the shallow pool?
2. How could you jump over the running pool in the gutter? What things might happen if someone rode his bicycle through the gutter while you were walking along? What things might be floating along the pool?
3. How would you react if you woke up at night to hear the "little sleep-song" on your roof? What might you do?

Thus, the leader might use the poem as a point of departure, but in and of itself, it is too much a "mood" piece to be of maximum effectiveness in drama.

By contrast, the delightfully alliterative poem below provides several images of children enjoying, perhaps surreptitiously, the joyful slooshes and sloshes, splishes and sploshes which the rain provides.

GALOSHES[13]

Susie's galoshes
Makes splishes and sploshes
And slooshes and sloshes
As Susie steps slowly
Along in the slush.

---

[12]This film (color, fifteen minutes, Churchill Films) is very helpful in setting the mood for some dramatic playing. It records the movement from the first few drops hitting the dried farmyard to the height of the storm as it moves to the city.

[13]From the book STORIES TO BEGIN ON by Rhoda W. Bacmeister. Copyright, 1940, by E. P. Dutton & Co., Inc. Renewal © 1968 by Rhoda W. Bacmeister. Published by E. P. Dutton & Co., Inc. and used with their permission. This is also available in *The Arbuthnot Anthology*, poetry section, p. 157.

> They stamp and they tramp
> On the ice and concrete,
> They get stuck in the muck and the mud;
> But Susie likes much best to hear
>
> The slippery slush
> As it slooshes and sloshes,
> And spliches and sploshes,
> All around her galoshes!

This poem, like "April Rain Song," provides word pictures, and children can learn to revel in the beauty of language typified by this type of poetry. However, it also provides—better than does the Hughes' poem—some concrete images for children to interpret. The images are limited, but the effective leader will quickly help children move beyond them by using his ability to question (which was discussed earlier).

Thus, the leader always asks himself what will children *do* as a result of this stimulus, not what will they be able to talk about. It is probable that a skilled leader will be able to adapt anything as motivation but, for the beginner, choosing poems or stories which give children something to do is probably a better idea.

One way to accomplish this is by selecting three or four possible pieces of literature for motivation and examining what kinds of verbs are present. You might ask yourself these questions:

1. How many verbs are included?
2. What kinds are they—active or passive?
3. Are they verbs *I* would be comfortable enacting?[14]
4. Are they verbs likely to suggest other active verbs children can use?

If your poem or story does not stand up well under such questioning, perhaps—especially if you are a beginner—you would be wise to set it aside for future use and search for a more "active" motivation.

Treatment of Material

After having selected a material, what does a leader do with it? How does he go about building a spontaneous drama session? New leaders share a common mistake: they frequently use too *much* material rather

---

[14]This is probably one of the best tests of material: "Can I do it myself?" If you cannot do it, e.g., if you would feel silly being a snowflake or a buttercup, perhaps you should choose another motivation.

than too little. An example of a very simple motivation is included here to demonstrate how even very slight ideas, if handled with imagination, can stimulate much valid improvising.

THE KING OF HEARTS[15]*

The queen of hearts,
    she made some tarts,
    all on a summer's day.

The knave of hearts,
    he stole the tarts,
    and he took them clean away.

The king of hearts,
    called for the tarts,
    and beat the knave full sore.

The knave of hearts,
    brought back the tarts,
    and vowed he'd steal no more.

Behind the deceptively uncomplicated lines of this rhyme lie many possibilities for discussion leading to playing. As one approach, the teacher might begin by asking children if they do something especially well, something of which they are very proud. He might discuss with children:

1. What is it you do well? When do you do it? With and/or for whom?
2. Did it take a long time to learn how to do this? What type of practice did you need?
3. How do you feel when you have done this? Satisfied? Can you describe your feeling of accomplishment?

Having established some interest in pride in things well done, the leader could then link the children's specialties with the queen's specialty: making tarts. At this point the leader begins questioning to get children to build on the very basic, unexpanded idea included in the rhyme:

1. Where had she learned to make these tarts?
2. Is this the only thing she can cook well, or has she other specialties as well?

---

[15]William Jay Smith, in *Laughing Time,* (Boston: Atlantic-Little, Brown and Co., 1955).
*The above treatment was outlined as a result of conversations with Mrs. Anne Thurman, director of creative dramatics, and Miss Dawn Murray of the Evanston (Illinois) public schools.

The "How" of Spontaneous Drama 53

3. Why is she making them on this particular day? (A child might suggest, for example, that she is making them because it is the king's birthday. This simple idea, or others, could lead to varied improvisations. If a different suggestion is made, the improvisation would follow in that direction.)

The rhyme, though short, allows much opportunity for characterization. Thinking about the queen, leader and children might discuss:

1. What is she like? Is she clever? Is she friendly?
2. What does she look like? Are there any other physical characteristics important about her?
3. What kind of a relationship does she have with the king? Is she domineering, sweet, reticent, overbearing, mild, or what? (One child suggested the queen was very crafty—with her skills she could get the king to agree to anything she wanted.)

Certainly the character of the king is a fruitful one for exploration. Many questions occur:

1. What is he like? Is he a pleasant person?
2. What has he done before we meet him that has made him the way he is? Is this his first wife?
3. What is his relationship to the queen? (One possibility might be that he is a gruff, crotchety king, who simply melts when his sweet young queen approaches him.)

The children could also do some interesting improvisations based around the knave. In one class, children suggested that the knave was the king's royal chef and explored these questions:

1. How secure is he in his job? Is he afraid he might lose his job? If so, why?
2. How does he behave to the other kitchen help, e.g., the salad girl, the pastry maker?
3. How does the knave like being interrupted by the queen?

In this situation, some sort of crisis could be developed. Exploring with children the effect the queen has on the smooth running of the kitchen can lead to some interesting conflict development:

1. What might go wrong while the queen makes her tarts? (Perhaps a child would suggest that some ingredient was missing, or perhaps a proper tart-making tool had been misplaced.)

2. How is this problem solved? *Is* it solved?
3. What if the queen got flustered working in a strange kitchen and did something wrong in the recipe?
4. What could happen if we discover that once the queen gets into the kitchen she really can't cook at all, that her reputation is a fabrication of her own making? How would she get out of her dilemma?

Other elements of the rhyme lead to plot and conflict development:

1. Who else might have wanted to steal the tarts? Why?
2. Where could they go so that they would not be discovered?
3. What might the queen do when she discovered that the tarts were gone?

Any number of playing possibilities might develop among children in responding to this crisis. Two are suggested, simply as ideas, not necessarily to be used as is with children:

1. The knave has stolen the tarts because he is anxious to make the queen lose favor with the king. Perhaps he is jealous because this beautiful young queen is influential, and the king no longer listens to the knave as much as he did before he married the queen.
2. Perhaps the knave is anxious to establish himself as an important person in the eyes of the people of the kingdom. There is to be a county fair soon, and he wants to enter the tarts as his own in the cooking contest, to win the prize and receive the glory.

The above is given as a rather general outline of some possibilities which exist within a short piece of literature.

After he has selected an appropriate material, thought about it, formulated questions related to it, and practiced reading or telling it (if it is a piece of literature), the teacher is then ready to use it with children. While he is actually "doing" drama with children, the teacher-leader has a rather carefully defined role to play.

The Leader's Role in the Drama Session

The danger in identifying stages is that it gives readers the impression that the stages can be divided; this is not the intent. I separated the two for easier examination of the leader's two different functions in the drama session.

Stage One: Teacher Participation

The inevitable question, and one difficult to answer, is: how much does the teacher participate? This is apparently impossible to answer without taking into consideration the context of a particular teacher and a particular group of children.

The *advantage* of participation is immediately evident. The children, seeing the leader actually taking part, will be moved to take part with more enthusiasm. If the leader is really bending and moving to the rhythmic impulses of the music, or stalking stealthily through the alley as the cat searching for a careless mouse, the children can enter wholeheartedly into the action. The tacit thought is: "He is doing it—so can I." By participating, the teacher is capitalizing on a child's desire to emulate, to follow the actions of a respected teacher. He is at that point acting the role of "cooperator" in the dramatic encounter, as Barnfield calls it.[16] That impulse, however, leads to a consideration of the drawback to teacher participation—the child's unconscious attempts to imitate or copy, not just the *spirit,* but the *letter* of the teacher's actions.

Children, particularly those who are unsure of themselves in the open, unstructured milieu of creative dramatics, may unconsciously seek approval by copying, movement for movement, the teacher's improvisation. Instead of getting *their* fresh ideas, the leader is apt to get a mirror image of *his* own ideas. This is farthest from his goal, as what he is after, encouraging, searching for, and rewarding is the child's *spontaneous* response to the stimulus. What then, is the teacher-leader to do? Can the quandry be resolved? Of course, it cannot be resolved, if by resolved one means a never-fail solution to the problem. There is, however, a generalization the leader may use to guide his behavior.

The teacher can remember that the only point in his participation is to *encourage* children, to show by concrete action that he believes this is an important learning activity. Therefore, as soon as it becomes apparent he has achieved this goal, he withdraws from active participation and moves, instead, to verbal encouragement. This takes no less ability, but does indeed remove the model so that those overly hesitant children, who find dependence on the model so hard to avoid, must move to more reliance on their own thoughts.

When does this occur? The apparent answer must be: at *different* times and with *different* speeds for *different* groups. With some drama groups it may happen before the end of the first session—and fortunate

---

[16]Barnfield, *Creative Dramatics in Schools,* op. cit., p. 20.

is the leader with so spontaneous a group of child improvisers. With another group it may take some time and, after he has established this hard won independence, the leader may at some later session again sense the children's hesitancy, wanting him to take part again. This is acceptable, providing he keeps in mind the real purpose of participation —to encourage the children.

That such a shift does occur, and that eventually the actual physical participation of the leader is unessential, has been apparent to me in working with groups of several different ages. Even in college students —many of whom are unbelievably stiff in so nonacademic a pursuit as dramatics—this need for encouragement by actual physical participation of the leader is apparent. In these future teachers, however, is also the need to do it themselves, and it soon becomes apparent that I am simply taking up floor space which should be put to a better use; so I withdraw to a corner and continue with the verbal encouragement.

It seems almost inevitable that the leader will want to participate, if for no other reason than that it demonstrates his conviction that the activity is a significant one. It is crucial, however, that he be aware of the need to withdraw from the action to a position of sideline support as soon as he senses growing independence on the part of the children.

Stage Two: Verbal Reinforcement

The second function is verbal—through questions and comments, the leader spurs children on, encourages the less sure ones, and points out strong ideas. To encourage children he says such things as:

> "I am really getting the feel of a jungle with all those crawling things wiggling and twisting around."
> "Such a lot of slippery fish I see, with their tails brushing from side to side —that stream is very full."

To encourage the less sure, he might make such comments as:

> "Now I can see the idea you have, Pam. It's coming through very nicely," or
> "Good, Bob, that stretching goes with our music so well."

To point out strong ideas he might say:

> "I can see Carol's cat is arching her back so slowly—it looks like it has just woke up," or
> "Did you see how Joe kept his arms and legs stiff? His toy soldier was very convincing."

The teacher's purpose in these oral comments is to further encourage the children. He is unconcerned if suddenly all the children become stiff-legged toy soldiers; soon, other ideas of their own will come to them.

The commentary needs always to be balanced. Some comments, or words of encouragement, are for the individual child who may need some private encouragement unimportant to the group. Then some comments are aimed at a particular child, pointing out what he or she is doing well, but also influencing the group. Finally, some comments are directed purposefully to the group in general, simply to convey approval, rather than to point out specific ideas to be emulated.

You will notice that in the above comments I have made use of specific children's names. Leaders vary in their reaction to this procedure. Certainly, further along in the series of drama sessions (for instance, when one is at work developing facets of character), it can destroy the session to call Carol, at work creating the old woman loaded down with parcels and waiting for a subway, by her right name. However, when the group is engaged in doing more fragmentary and less sustained impressions, personalization—and this is especially true for younger children—and supportive comments cannot be anything but helpful.

Both leader participation and verbal reinforcement have a single purpose—that of building such a sense of security in children that they will feel totally free to say or do whatever seems appropriate to them in the improvisation.

Gaining Freedom of Response

As stated earlier, the leader's intense belief in this art form as beneficial is necessary, as it encourages the children's honest responses. Getting such an honest response from children to the stimulus for the day may be more difficult than the leader anticipates, especially if he is trying to begin spontaneous dramatics with an older group of children for the first time.

The one startling characteristic adults notice often about very young children is their frankness or honesty. Ask any kindergarten teacher—he will tell you that (with the exception, unfortunately, of a few children from repressive backgrounds) his charges are most typically characterized by a forthrightness seldomly encountered elsewhere. The children both ask questions and state their opinions with a disconcerting candor. Similarly, their imagination or dramatic sense is, at an early age, relatively unfettered. Their creativity is matched in vigor only by their eagerness to use it.

Somewhere, somehow, before typical children leave a typical elementary school, most of this creativity, this spontaneity, this daring to adventure is either lost or repressed. Why? Several psychologists have advanced answers, and readers interested in the problem might examine the materials by Heinrich.[17]

For our purposes here it is sufficient to note the problem, and then go on to say simply that the leader may have a difficult time getting children to unbend enough to react spontaneously to a motivation. Often children have been conditioned to look to the teacher for the idea and, after following the lead he gives, to look to him again for reinforcement that something has been done correctly.

To the spontaneous drama leader this is anathema. He is interested in getting children to respond openly. To get this freedom, he may have to accept for some time attempts which he knows are not open, free responses, but rather a young child's attempt to figure out what he wants. At times he will need to be careful not to criticize a particular child's obviously false behavior and be simply content to ask again—in a group or, perhaps, individually—"Is that what you *really* feel?"

I recently worked with a beginning teacher of third grade who demonstrated in his handling of an informal play-giving situation obvious insensitivity to the possibilities in that dramatic situation. Each of his reading groups had devised an activity, a way of sharing the story they were studying with the rest of the class. One group had chosen to "do" a play based on the story. When they stood up in front of the class, the players, some of whom tried to hide behind others, giggled and shoved each other in embarrassment and read their parts poorly, with little expression. Once they began, the children, with one exception, stood frozen to the spot and even minimal movement, e.g., answering the door, was absent. A song, to be sung by six children, was mumbled through in an uninteresting monotone, though the words were set to a melody every school child knows. All in all, it was a total waste of children's time! There were a myriad of possibilities present in this informal dramatic situation, but there was only time to do the play once, as spelling was next on the agenda.

Certainly, the teacher needed to consider the following:

1. Since there was no continuing program of drama in the room, the children needed supervised help in practicing their play. The children were not used to such activities and, though they

---

[17]See: June Sark Heinrich, *Creativity in the Classroom* (SRA Teacher Education Extension Service) (Chicago: Science Research Associates, 1967), p. 14 ff. An unusual in-service learning project, this publication deals generally with creativity and includes an especially helpful checklist for teachers to use in analyzing their own creativity.

voluntarily chose to share their story in this way, they needed help in doing it.
2. As the children were not used to dramatizing with an audience watching, some provision might have been made for the group to present their play to one reading group at a time, rather than to all the rest of the children. For most children small audiences are less formidable than class-size groups.
3. Some provision needed to be made for evaluation. Probably in this case, such evaluation needed to be done when the teacher had some time to speak privately with the group. The fact that some evaluation was going on among the children is evidenced by the next paragraph.

Perhaps the most interesting happening was an exchange between a young boy who was sitting next to me and myself. In a silly attempt to make small talk, I said to him: "Did you enjoy the play?" His candor was evident: "No—it wasn't very interesting." He then proceeded to make three suggestions which would have, indeed, improved the improvised play—the child would have made a better leader at that point than the actual teacher had! The child had been concentrating on the dramatic qualities of the idea and in a noncritical way had identified some possibilities the self-conscious "performers" had ignored.

Somehow we too frequently condition children and their teachers to expect particular types of activities in elementary schools. As a result, freer and less-structured experiences, in which children can experiment with ideas and try out their thoughts in informal, oral situations, seem silly—if not impossible. The self-conscious children in this example, given the opportunity to develop their own ideas, instead made stilted and lifeless use of the author's ideas. They were too inhibited to add anything of themselves because they were not ready to dramatize for an audience, though the situation had much potential.

John Holt, in a stimulating book, has described this utter dependence and overly conventionalized behavior and a child's disbelief when confronted with the need to exercise independence and make choices. Though he is not talking about drama, the following illustration makes the point well. He is describing a situation in which he gave the children a choice of what they were to read and told them he did not intend to either quiz them on what they had read or make them give book reports on the books.

> The children sat stunned and silent. Was this a teacher talking? One girl . . . who proved to be one of the most lively and intelligent children I have ever known, looked at me steadily for a long time after I had

finished. Then, still looking at me, she said slowly and solemnly, "Mr. Holt, do you really mean that?"[18]

Is there really any wonder that, confronted with children who have been so conditioned to expect a particular type of situation in school, some of us feel it is imperative that we offer children an opportunity to express themselves through drama?

How Does One Begin With Children?

The problem of how to present the idea of spontaneous dramatics differs according to the age group with which one is working. In the early primary grades a *direct approach* is quite possible, i.e., the leader simply begins the activity; there is no need to talk about it. He can begin simply with rhythmic activities to music or, after reading a poem, he can encourage children to show how the action took place. For children at this level life is simpler—activity is pleasurable for its own sake—and resistance to the idea will be minimal.

In her series of videotapes,[19] using middle-grade children, Crist uses a different approach, that of talking with children first about ideas and how they can be expressed. Gradually she moves to the concept of expressing ideas with one's body and, thus, leads into the concept of spontaneous dramatics.

At any level beyond third grade an *analytical approach* is undoubtedly necessary, i.e., one needs to talk with children about what one is going to do with them, and why, and allow them much opportunity to discuss the idea, think about it, and react to it before beginning.

Some leaders have found that much work with rhythmic movement is a good lead into dramatics, no matter what the level. The book by Andrews[20] gives many positive suggestions for ways to loosen up

---

[18]John Holt, *The Underachieving School* (New York: Pitman Publishing Co., 1969), p. 86. Holt's seventeen years of teaching experience at a variety of levels have made him an acute observer and a trenchant commentator on the ills which infect American schools. Many of his comments are startling (see his chapter on the need to abolish compulsory attendance laws); some are merely common sense we have ignored (comments on the problem besetting reading programs). A refreshingly contentious book which will make you think in new ways about continuing problems.

[19]Rita Crist, *All That I Am*, op. cit.

[20]Gladys Andrews, *Creative Rhythmic Movement for Children* (Englewood Cliffs, N.J. Prentice-Hall, 1954). Mrs. Andrews, concerned with movement exercises which can be done in an ordinary classroom, describes in helpful fashion how to begin doing rhythmic activities with children. The section on sitting movements is unusual, as are those on the relationship between art and movement and on spatial relationships. The book, which includes much piano music of use in motivating specific types of movements, also includes a list of resources and a bibliography which is a complete guide to older materials.

children, and to give them an understanding of what their bodies can convey and of ways to remove inhibitions. Though Mrs. Andrews remains primarily concerned with movement for its own sake, drama leaders find the book of much help to them in beginning work with children.

Drama leaders will also find the Barnfield book full of suggestions about ways to begin.[21] His book is particularly encouraging for those interested in doing drama with older children, because the work he reports was done with groups of boys between ten and fourteen years of age. In addition to suggestions for introducing this activity to children for the first time, he also includes some stimulating loosening-up exercises for relaxing the body (and consequently the mind) at the beginning of each session.

A description of how I begin an actual session in spontaneous drama with older children might be of interest. I usually use the material found in Chapter 5 on "The Sandhill Crane" (page 115) and, when the students enter, the room is dark—the only light is from a slide of the crane showing on the screen. We talk briefly about the crane, including the fact that his wingspread is nine feet from one tip to the other. Then, sitting on the floor, we stretch our arms out until we feel the tingle which comes to the ends of our fingertips when we stretch as far as we can. We then begin to move our upper torsos around, while remaining sitting. We stretch as far in all directions as we can, retaining the feeling of the wide wingspread. Commenting continuously on the tingle, and the size of their "wings," I encourage them to get up and to move around, to see what kinds of problems being that size entails. As they move and interrelate in the space, the mood begins to establish itself and, when we sit down on our nests some minutes later, the children have changed—if not into cranes, at least into beings more able to forget themselves and work with the ideas presented. It is only after this introductory movement session of perhaps five minutes that we begin to consider other aspects of the poem and begin to work out what happens in the course of the poem. Such is the introduction which has worked well with intermediate-age students, very unused to expressing their thoughts with their bodies in a classroom situation.

The foregoing is certainly not an effective prescription for exactly how to begin drama with children. Such is impossible for, as an author, I do not know either you or your group of children. Intelligent decision making about the kinds of drama experiences a particular group of students needs can only be done when a leader is able to look analytically at his group. He tries to determine what they have done, what he

---

[21]Barnfield, *Creative Dramatics in Schools*, op. cit.

hopes they will eventually be able to do, and what types of activities may help them toward achieving these goals. These determinations are always made within the context of his own strengths and weaknesses as a leader. Since I know neither you nor your group, all I can do is to encourage you to read this, and anything else you can find, and then try to diagnose the drama needs of your group.

Essential Drama Elements

Both in choosing materials to use in spontaneous dramatics and in working with children the leader keeps in mind three elements which are necessary to good drama.

Conflict

The element which most often makes stories and plays of interest is some sort of conflict. The most beautiful sets and dialogue, or the most effectively written descriptions, rarely hold even an attentive audience for long. The playright or author needs to establish some conflict. In addition to being good drama, a fact of secondary interest to us, conflict is essential in spontaneous drama sessions.

Children can enter into this conflict with gusto, for as Sendak says: "Being defenseless is a primary attribute of childhood."[22] Children enjoy acting out their feelings of defenselessness through the acceptable vehicle of drama sessions which are concerned with conflict.

There are three types of conflict which have been identified by drama writers, and examples of all three are to be found in stories for children. First, there is the conflict of *man versus man.* An example of this type is the conflict between the fisherman and his avaricious wife, in the story by the same title.[23]

A second type is the conflict of *man versus fate,* i.e., nature, the supernatural, or something larger than himself. An example of this type is found in the old Italian folk tale about the overly confident shepherd.[24] The wily shepherd contends against the stronger force, the month, but finally loses.

In the third type of conflict—*man versus himself*—it is some internal flaw in his character which propels the character toward disaster. An

---

[22]Nat Hentoff, "Among the Wild Things" *New Yorker* (January 22, 1966), p. 39 ff. (See annotation, included in Chapter 6, p. 150).

[23]"The Fisherman and His Wife," in the folk tales section of Arbuthnot's anthology, op. cit., p. 56.

[24]"March and the Shepherd," folk tale section of Arbuthnot's anthology, op. cit., p. 129.

example of this type is the tale of the willful chick whose callous indifference to the needs of others eventually leads to his downfall.[25]

Characterization

The problem of how to make people or animals real is a continuing one. The leader's goal in dramatization is to get an honest interpretation of the character from the child. There are several things to be kept in mind in trying to achieve this goal.

First, he selects characters which meet certain requirements. Many writers agree that, generally, the characters appropriate for dramatic improvisations share three qualities:

1. *They are active, not passive.* Either the king or Bartholomew are good examples of this characteristic, as drawn in the story by Seuss.[26] Bartholomew is actively involved through most of the story in escaping his perplexing problems, while the King is also equally active in attempting to punish what he sees as Bartholomew's insolence.

2. *They are clearly defined.* As an example of this quality, "Mrs. Wallaby-Jones" serves very well. In the section included below, a very evocative picture of this extraordinary woman is created for the reader.[27]

> The lady's speech was rather different from their own, and Jill had heard her mother say once that the English went in for hyphenated names. Mrs. Wallaby-Jones had mentioned her hyphen when she introduced herself, as if she considered it a mark of distinction.
>
> She sounded distinctly huffy, and as they watched she seemed to grow about two feet taller. Maybe she was swelling with rage about something —they had heard about that, though they had never seen it happen. They wondered anxiously what could have upset her.
>
> She pointed to Mrs. Wallaby-Jone's footprints in the light snow. They certainly were enormous for a lady. "I never saw any like that before, and her hands are smaller than mine."
>
> There was Mrs. Wallaby-Jones, sitting as prim as ever in her sleek fur coat and her fur hat and tippet, her gloved hands folded in her lap. But she had pulled up her skirt just a trifle, probably to keep it dry. And underneath,

---

[25]The old Spanish folk tale is entitled, "The Half Chick," folk tale section of Arbuthnot's anthology, op. cit., p. 131. Children enjoy dramatizing this old tale, in which the overconfident chick ignores opportunities to be of service. Children find his eventual come-uppance, when the others are too busy to help him, a delightful form of poetic retribution.

[26]Dr. Seuss, *The 500 Hats of Bartholomew Cubbins* (New York: Vanguard Press, 1938).

[27]Joan Howard, *The 13th is Magic* (New York: Lothrop, Lee & Shepard, 1950).

hanging over the back of the little rowboat and acting as a rudder, was something—something—Jill and Ronnie were not sure what it was, but it certainly did look like the tip of a Kangaroo's tail.

3. *They are logically motivated.* Even within the context of fantasy, characters can act and behave logically—they need not exhibit realistic behavior to be believable. The delightful story entitled "The Picnic Basket,"[28] provides a fine example, as it is simple for children to understand both the dilatory behavior of Andrewshek and why Auntie Katushka acts as she does. They are very logical and believable people.

In addition to selecting materials which include appropriate characterizations, the leader works during the session to increase the children's concentration on the characters under consideration. He is concerned with three types of concentration:

1. *Intellectual*—Are you thinking like the person would think?
2. *Emotional*—Are you feeling like the person would feel?
3. *Physical*—Are you moving, standing, or sitting like the person would?

Barnfield describes his approach in getting children to *become* characters rather than "act" them, a very important distinction.

> Let them start their scene and let it run for a minute. Now stop them and ask one of them what his name is. He may look puzzled, then give you his own name. "No," you will say, "Who are you in this scene?" He probably hasn't thought. Ask another, and another and you will find that their imagination has been very general in its working. Now, explain to them "I want you to think who you are: how old or young, man or woman, school boy or school girl, when your next birthday is and what age you will be then. Are you poor or fairly well off? What kind of clothes are you wearing—What are you carrying ... Are you with anyone ..." With all these suggestions let them have another try at their ... scene.[29]

Dialogue

Some drama leaders believe that dialogue is, logically enough, one of the last elements to develop. They believe that a child first develops an

---

[28]by Margery Clark, included in "Today in the United States" section of Arbuthnot's anthology, op. cit., p. 91.

[29]Barnfield, *Creative Dramatics in Schools,* op. cit. pp. 98–99.

image in his mind (as a result of the motivation), then this image stimulates actions, and only finally evokes dialogue.

Certainly anyone who has worked with children is aware of their apparent muteness in many situations where other children are listening. Both Canadian and British drama leaders attempt to solve this problem by making use of *simultaneous speech*, either individually or in small groups, to break down the child's reticence at hearing his own voice. This is, in some external aspects, similar to the ancient practice of Chinese children reciting aloud in school simultaneously.

The procedure, which will seem like chaos in the beginning, is simple to initiate and is recommended here because of its effectiveness. One may begin with single child dialogue; the children position themselves in the room, the leader provides a motivation in a situation which requires a verbal response of some nature, and each child creates spontaneous dialogue of his own, saying it aloud and ignoring all the other children.

For example, the leader could use the character of mother rabbit in Beatrix Potter's stories about Peter Rabbit and set the stage for the children to improvise the warnings mother rabbit might have given to her children before sending them out to play. Each child becomes the mother rabbit, and each makes up a warning, ignoring the rest of the children within the room. For older children the leader might try having them improvise on their father's reaction to a bad report card. Both Canadian and British drama leaders report informally that greatly increased oral fluency results from these sessions, but in this, as in most aspects of drama, empirical research is limited.

Another approach, which I have found to work equally well, is to divide the children into small groups (of not more than four) and have them create dialogue spontaneously as a result of some motivation. Working in this intimate group, and thus concentrating intently on what the others in their group are saying, children quickly forget the presence of others in the room and concentrate on improvising their dialogue.

We have, with good effect, used the unfinished stories included in *Today's Education* as motivation for activities of this kind. They provide conflict situations usually involving a small number of people and adapt easily to this use.[30]

One can, if desired, progress from individual monologues to small group dialogues and continually increase the size of the group, gradually

---

[30]Though intended as motivation for creative writing, this series of stories, one of which is included in each issue of *Today's Education*, is a good resource for the drama leader.

lessening the children's self-consciousness in speaking with others and making the creation of spontaneous dialogue seem easy.

Redoing the Improvisation

One of the recurring themes in this book has been that to any motivation there will be, if encouraged, a variety of responses from the children. Stimulated by an idea, challenged by the skillful questioning of the leader, children will be eager to share their responses. The leader does not choose which of these he thinks is "best," but rather, will frequently allow different groups of children to show their response to an idea, or he may let the total group respond several times to the same motivation. He may do this for several reasons.

1. To give all children a chance to participate. In the story of *The Ginger Bread Boy*,[31] for instance, the basic characters are few. Though children will undoubtedly be able to suggest other peripheral characters which can be added to the story, the total number will probably be less than the number of children in the group, thus necessitating dramatizing the story more than once.

2. To work on different dramatic aspects possible in a motivation. In a story of *Jack and the Beanstalk*,[32] one could work on characterization, plot extension and development, or mood, and the story probably should be done more than once in order to concentrate on these different aspects.

3. To "set" an improvisation, when children have expressed a desire to do it for another group of children. This term is used to describe the process of doing a number of improvisations on the same theme, and selecting the better ideas and rejecting the poorer ones. The purpose of this procedure is to build a dramatic piece to be learned, which will yet retain the freshness of the original spontaneous idea. It should be remembered that this does not happen at the beginning of a sequence of drama experiences when we are interested in encouraging diversity of

---

[31]While doing this story (available in Arbuthnot's anthology, op. cit.) in dramatics, the teacher can make some meaningful correlation by reading other versions of the old folk tale to children. The ones included in Virginia Haviland, *Favorite Fairy Tales Told in England* (Boston: Little, Brown, and Co., 1959), p. 22, and Veronica S. Hutchinson, *Chimney Corner Stories* (New York: Minton, Balch and Co., 1925), p. 19, are quite different than the one found in Arbuthnot's anthology. See also the unique version included in *A Curriculum for English* (Lincoln: The University of Nebraska Press, 1966), grade 1, p. 2.

[32]The illustrations by William Stobbs in *Jack and the Beanstalk* (New York: Delacorte Press, 1965) are good to use in motivating interest in the story. Though only two-color, they include a suitably fearsome giant and wily Jack in illustrations so exuberant they scarcely can be contained on the page.

response. After children have worked in drama for some time, they may want to "set" the improvisation, so it can be done for another group of children.

Thus, we see there may be several occasions when children will work more than once with the same basic motivational idea.

Each time this happens the improvisation is at least slightly different from what went before, and this quality is encouraged by the leader. Perhaps this quality can be most graphically illustrated by drawing a parallel between the variety in drama and in a piece of music. Listen, for example, to Rachmaninoff's *Rhapsody on a Theme of Paganini* (Seraphim S-60091). In this piece the composer has taken a short melodic idea and given it back to the listener in twenty-two variations, each different enough so that the listener follows from one to the other with increasing interest. Given a basic idea, he has shown us the infinite variety possible.

In a similar fashion, if the spontaneous dramatics leader is effective, each time a group works with an idea the results will be different. Though he is by no means interested in doing anything twenty-two times, the leader will often need to play the idea more than once, and each time it is done it will turn out to be slightly different. The teacher capitalizes on this and encourages such differences, as part of developing the creativity of the children.

Evaluation of the Session

The final aspect of a spontaneous drama session is at least as crucial as the rest of the steps, for it involves assessing what happened during the session.

Using the term evaluation necessitates careful definition. Often simple grading of past performance has been called evaluation; in some instances, it means the teacher *discusses* with children their work, as opposed to *writing* an "evaluation." In dramatics, however, evaluation is used to mean a very different type of activity, the major feature of which is its cooperative nature, *truly* cooperative.

By cooperative we mean that both children and leader share their reactions when confronted with the question: how did *we* do today? The teacher *leads* the discussion after the children have improvised, but he does not *manipulate* it—a crucial distinction. The leader asks such questions as:

1. Which were the best parts of our improvisation? What things helped to make the story clear? Could people follow what was happening?

2. What parts of it could be improved? How could we convey our idea more clearly?
3. Which characters were most believable? What aspects made them believable?
4. How did the dialogue help to make the story live? What made it interesting? Was there enough dialogue, but not so much that it got to be mainly talk?
5. What could we do to make it better next time? What are some of the things we did today that we will want to remember to do again next time?

The teacher probably does two types of evaluation. One, the supportive comments, is spontaneous on his part and points out the good aspects during playing. This type of evaluation was mentioned earlier. The second type is our present concern, the *cooperative group evaluation* done at the end of the session. When the period is drawing to a close, the leader will bring the children back together, perhaps by having them sit in a circle near him, as proximity is helpful. Then they begin to discuss what went on during the session, the leader remembering always to draw ideas from the children and being careful not to say too much himself, so that the children don't begin to try to guess what they "should" say. The teacher naturally is not limited to the questions included above—they are simply given as examples.

There is a natural pitfall involved in this procedure—the teacher-leader unconsciously communicates his own ideas without identifying them as such. In question one (above), for example, what he sees as "best about the day's work" might conceivably be quite different from what the children view as "best," perhaps because he misunderstood the intent of what the children were trying to accomplish. At this stage in the session it is imperative that the teacher's listening skills, as mentioned earlier, be used as intensively as they were while the children were actually working out their ideas during the session. He may learn something about children's ideas related to the motivation, or to what they were trying to do, which could be of help during the next session. All of this emphasis on careful listening to children, and on accepting their effort, does not suggest a bland acquiesence in mediocrity, insincerity, or superficial praise of everything children do.

Praise and Honesty

The leader is always careful to avoid praising unjustly, for children will know when they have done something that is good. The teacher who, for whatever reason, intellectually or artistically deceives the children by excessive or inappropriate praise inevitably loses his group. Knowing that he accepts anything, regardless of its quality, children lose their interest and, thus, their desire to participate. The teacher must come to grips with inadequate effort; he avoids both defeating excessive praise and censorious teacher-evaluation by seeking to establish a healthy rapport with his children. This is a rapport in which leader and children can investigate together what has been done, what was done well, and what needs to be done better.

I cannot resist sharing with you my own feeling that a few minutes away from the children after the session is crucial for the leader. Drama is not a sedentary process—the leader (if effective) has concentrated intently and has been active physically; therefore, he needs a few minutes to regather his forces. A more crucial purpose of this brief respite is to jot down a few brief notes, for himself alone, which will help give continuity to the sessions as a *sequence* of drama experiences. Because it is almost inevitable that a few days will elapse before the next session occurs, the leader will find that a few notes jotted down about the day's session will help him to remember what he wants to do in the next session. In the interval—spent helping with such diverse problems as the addition of equal addends, and the expansion of air molecules—the memory of the previous drama session will become hazy, or nonexistent. Looking back at these minimal notes will refresh his memory of what the group did, what it needs to do again, and what it did not get to do. These few indications surely do not take the place of a sequential drama plan, but serve to augment it, to bridge the gap between plan and reality.

As the leader will find problems of sequence, so he will also find problems of space. Doing drama in an ordinary elementary school classroom setting is not simple. As both a college methods professor and supervisor of student teachers, I frequently hear the question: "I like the *idea* of drama, but how do I do it with thirty children in my classroom?" Perhaps the suggestions which follow may be of help.

Physical Problems: What to Do?

The teacher faces a myriad of problems in his attempt to do spontaneous drama with his classroom. The first of these is probably the number of pupils which have been assigned to him. Recommendations of optimum group size for drama vary, but whatever the recommendations, it is apparent that few classroom teachers normally operate with classes this small. It is a rare and gifted leader, and seldom a beginning one, who can be totally effective with thirty children. Therefore, your first job is to reduce your thirty children to a smaller number for efficient playing.

70   The "How" of Spontaneous Drama

What will you do to accomplish this? Following are some suggestions tried by leaders interested in working in creative drama.

1. Let the part of the group you are not working with go to a corner of the room and do something else. The key here is *seclusion*. Perhaps a folding screen, moveable shelves, or a piano on rollers could provide a secluded corner in the room. A second key to success is to have these children doing something pleasurable. Engrossed in a compelling story *they* chose to read, their attention is less likely to wander than if they are doing makeup math lessons. After the first group has its turn, switch groups.

2. Find another place to send some of the children.
   a. Could you work out a flexible scheduling for art, music, and physical education classes? Perhaps half of your children, plus half of the teacher's next door, could go together for art. This would give the art teacher a full class, but give each of you only half a class.
   b. Is there a way the children could help around the school? Could one group regularly read stories to younger children, or perhaps help with spelling drill in another room? Making such an arrangement with another teacher not only helps the children, but allows the teacher to do more individualization. Another possibility is making an arrangement with the librarian to have her use part of your group as helpers. In addition, perhaps the school office could make use of some helpers on a regular basis. Any or all of these techniques allow you to reduce the size of the group remaining in your room to one small enough to work with.

3. Enlist the aid of some additional workers.
   a. Working under your direction, a mother can become a second leader. One short planning session per week, after she has had several weeks to watch you work with the children, can inform her of what she is to do that particular week. Let her take half of the children to the gym, cafeteria, or any other convenient space and work with them while you work with the rest. Another possibility is to enlist the help of teacher aides, if your school employs such auxiliary personnel. In considering this suggestion and the next one, the teacher will need to check on state laws regarding responsibility for children. These laws vary greatly concerning the use of such paraprofessional help.
   b. Another possible source of auxiliary personnel is a college or university in the area. People operating programs in creative

drama at this level are frequently hard pressed for placement opportunities for students enrolled in their courses. They would usually be delighted to put one of their students in your classroom. Programs vary, but it is a rare college which would not be pleased to provide more actual contact hours with children for students in programs of this nature and, in setting up something like this, you both benefit. Don't wait for the college instructor to come to you—initiate the contact yourself, and you are sure to be pleased with the response.

The second problem is one of space, and it is often a discouraging one. Two comments are related to this:

1. If you are going to use your classroom (which fortunately has moveable desks), children will need practice in clearing the desks from the middle of the room. You will need to plan ahead where each desk should go in order to get the largest amount of open space; then, children will need to practice clearing the area (and restoring it back to normal) *several times,* in order to get the best movement of desks in the least amount of time with a minimum of confusion and noise. This can be done, as any teacher who has tried to overcome physical problems can tell you. But it does *not* "happen" automatically and can *easily* dissolve in chaos, unless you think about the process before you try it.

2. There may be an unused space somewhere in the building which you could use. Get the gym teacher's schedule to find out when that space is available. Ask when the cafeteria workers finish so you could use that space. Is there an art or music room unused for some part of the week? Look around—sometimes the most unsuspected spaces will do for a while! These are not ideal, as they may control your scheduling of drama sessions, but it is my —and I hope by now, your—feeling that good drama experiences can take place in poor locations. Once you have the drama program launched and children are spreading the word about it, you may be able to come up with a better space.

The final problem usually encountered is the scheduling problem. The stereotyped idea of the teacher handing out crayons and paper and telling children to "draw what you want to" on Friday afternoons from 3:00 to 3:30 p.m. is, unfortunately, still too true to suit most art educators. Most children cannot create at the end of the week. (Most researchers agree that when people are either physically or mentally tired they tend to be less creative.) Similarly, spontaneous drama, being essentially an activity in which the child is expressing or "giving out," rather than impressing or "taking in," also cannot wait until the child is physically and mentally exhausted. No one can create then. If the only time of the week you can "spare" from a busy schedule is that last period of the day or week, perhaps you should reexamine the priorities.

1. Who is establishing for you what you should teach, and when?
2. Is what the teacher in the next grade "expects" your children to have learned a legitimate expectation? If not, what should you be doing to change it?
3. Just exactly what are the expectations of your principal? How do you know? Has he said so, or do you "think" he expects certain things?
4. Do your children really "need" an hour of prime time in the middle of each morning devoted to arithmetic? How do you know? Who should establish what children "need"? Can we determine these needs, especially subject matter ones, with much certainty?

An interesting revelation to me was the comment made recently during a conversation with a school principal in Minneapolis, Minnesota. In her school they are experimenting with behavioral modification techniques, and the tangible reward offered is a half-hour "free" period at the end of the day, during which children choose from several activities. Though this entailed shortening the academic school day—in essence, curtailing the amount of time for academic "teaching"—the principal reported that children did as well or better on the standardized achievement tests at the end of the first year of the experiment as they did the previous year when the teachers had the extra half-hour each day to teach! Perhaps we waste more of the children's time than we think we do! Time for drama can usually be found, providing the teacher wants to find the time.

Now that we have discussed at some length the "how" of spontaneous drama, we have left only one brief topic—how do you convince your school system that spontaneous drama is a good idea?

Selling the Idea to a School System

While the teacher himself may be convinced of the need to include dramatics, the social understandings which children gain from doing drama are too frequently not of interest to those planning and controlling curriculum. Though the schools in America give lip service to independence, self-expression, social self-confidence, and other "self-oriented" goals, there is enough evidence to suggest that these do not, in fact, figure largely in the planning of most school people. We must admit that such factors as these are almost impossible to measure. Apparently, one either accepts such factors as important and works from this philosophical position, or gives lip service only to the ideas and demonstrates that his major interests lie elsewhere.

The teacher must be aware that he *will* need to sell the idea, and conscious planning for his sales pitch will be necessary.

1. He talks about this idea with whoever will listen. This includes talking with other teachers informally in the teacher's room, with the principal in his office, and even with parents as he encounters them casually in the supermarket.[33]
2. He presents ideas in formal situations, i.e., he is willing to put forth the effort to prepare a talk about drama for the school board, for the principals' meeting, for the teachers' meeting, or for the parent-teacher meeting—if such activities will help convince people of the benefits of drama.
3. He may wish to communicate with parents in writing. Some drama leaders send home letters periodically reporting on the drama sessions in order to keep parents informed.

Part of the job of "selling" a spontaneous drama program is taken care of by the children, whose enthusiastic comments about the program once it is underway will help inform adults of the benefits of such a program. But, the teacher-leader can never rely upon such informal and unplanned publicity for the program. Rather, he should consciously analyze the people he is trying to convince of the value of a drama program, identifying what approach will appeal to them *and* what problems they may anticipate and arguments he may have to marshall to deal with these. It is by such conscious analysis and then by equally conscious efforts at publicizing his program that the enthusiastic drama leader enlists the support he needs to make the program a success.

---

[33]The ability to do this depends, naturally enough, on the teacher's infectious enthusiasm for what he is doing. Though this has not been mentioned consciously, it is an assumed quality in the teacher. See: "Teachers: The Need and the Task" for a convincing statement of the importance of the teacher being "turned on" about what he is doing. (Ninth Annual Charles W. Hunt Lecture, by Felix C. Robb, given at the 1968 meeting of American Association of Colleges of Teacher Education, Chicago. Copies available from the association).

Summary

In this chapter we have investigated some important factors related to the implementation of a drama program. The leader, being central to the success of such a program, needs to be flexible, to be a good question asker, to believe in the dramatic experience, and to be aware of the various stages in his participation. Some very specific suggestions were included as to how to plan a session, including getting an honest response from children, selecting material, and developing conflict and character. Some attention was given to evaluating the sessions, to dealing with physical problems, and to "selling" the idea of drama to a school system. It is hoped that with this rather extensive chapter on the "how" of drama, if you are interested in beginning dramatics with children, you will be encouraged enough to forge ahead. The following chapter includes an examination of the specific language learnings which can occur as a result of drama experiences. This should give you some further ideas about how to convince people of the values of such a program.

4

Drama as a Language Art

On the basis of observation, it is possible to question the importance of dramatics in elementary classrooms in the United States. Unlike the case in British infant schools,[1] where drama plays an integral role throughout the entire school, spontaneous dramatics remains on the periphery of the curriculum in our schools.

Five years of observing over 150 classrooms in three states have led me to the conclusion that too many classroom teachers cannot find the time to give more than fleeting attention to dramatic activities or cannot convince authorities of the value of such activities.

Perhaps few teachers try to do drama with children because they receive so little support for such activities from two influential sources which determine the curriculum—the textbook and the curriculum guide. An *Instructor* magazine survey, conducted in 1965, indicated that for 81.5 percent of the teachers surveyed, the source of the curriculum was the textbook. Obviously, then, textbooks frequently control what is taught to a large degree. How do textbooks treat dramatic activities? Do they deal with such activities at all?

An analysis of content and emphases in elementary language arts series textbooks concluded:

> [although editors and writers] ... state explicitly and imply that oral communication should be stressed ... Nevertheless, actual emphasis in the books does not support this.[2]

---

[1] Peter Harris, ed., "Drama in Education," *English in Education* 1, no. 3, Autumn 1967 (London: Bodley Head).

[2] Kenneth L. Brown, "Speech and Listening in Language Arts Textbooks," *Elementary English* 44 (April 1967), pp. 336–341.

Brown studied fourteen different language arts series and, although he was concerned with *all* oral activities rather than only with spontaneous dramatics, he found that: "... it is apparent that writing and grammar are emphasized more than speaking and listening."[3] This emphasis is in spite of numerous studies which point conclusively to the fact that such conscious teaching of grammar yields a very small return for time expended.[4]

The careful analysis done by Brown indicated that language arts textbooks gave little attention to conscious teaching of oral skills. He concluded:

> There is a tendency to regard any oral activity as a lesson in speech. Participating alone in speaking and listening assignments does not assure development of effective speech and listening skills.[5]

Although Brown's study is by now an older one, it has not been replicated. In new language arts materials, revised content and emphases generally place greater priority on oral language activities; however, the question of how successful they have been in encouraging drama remains unanswered.

Another influential source on what is taught is the curriculum guide, and Davidson's examination of these led her to the conclusion that such guides give very limited support to a teacher interested in beginning a drama program with children. She concludes:

> None of the guides attach the importance to ... drama ... as a teaching method, and do not suggest the need for a detailed ... sequence in drama which moves from ... improvising language and movement to exploring in action the meaning of a script. ...[6]

More recent than Brown's study, Davidson's analysis reinforces our suspicion that the teacher apparently gets little encouragement from either language arts textbooks or curriculum guides, the two major determinants of the curriculum, in his efforts to establish a program of drama experiences.

---

[3]Brown, *Elementary English,* op. cit., p. 341.

[4]A very complete summary of all the research studies which establish conclusively that grammar skill is unrelated to other language skills is included in Harry A. Greene and Walter T. Petty, *Developing Language Skills in the Elementary Schools,* 4th ed. (Boston: Allyn & Bacon, 1971), pp. 372–375.

[5]Brown, *Elementary English,* op. cit.

[6]Dorothy Davidson, "Trends in Curriculum Guides," *Elementary English* 45 (November 1968), pp. 891–897.

Reasons for Lack of Emphasis

The reasons why dramatic activities have been largely ignored are rather difficult to determine, especially in view of the cogent and convincing statements made about the values of drama by its proponents.

A search of the literature in this area reveals many clear and concise statements of the social and emotional values gained by including drama in the elementary curriculum. Geraldine Brain Siks, a respected authority in the field, speaks specifically of five values.[7] These include:

1. Social development
2. Creative self-expression
3. Wholesome emotional development
4. Attitudes and appreciations
5. Development of inner security

Mrs. Siks and other drama leaders have for many years been describing in detail such psychological gains as these. While it is not the intent to minimize such gains, we need to be aware that many critics of education charge that such social-emotional concerns are not of fundamental interest to educators. Silberman is the latest in a succession of educational critics who make us, through their acerbic but accurate accusations, reexamine what we believe.[8]

In addition to the statements of social-emotional values, we can find other equally convincing statements by classroom teachers about the values they have found in using dramatics as a tool to teach other subject matter. Writers have pointed out how drama can help teach reading, history, and social studies.[9]

Despite the identification of both emotional values and subject matter applications, the problem remains; drama has found itself in the same tenuous position as have the arts and foreign language instruction.

---

[7]"Perceiving Through Creative Dramatics," in *English Encountered* (a service bulletin), ed. Miss V. Littlefield. (Madison, Wisc.: Wisconsin Department of Public Instruction, no. 3, February 1968).

[8]Charles Silberman, "Murder in the Schoolroom," *The Atlantic* (June, July, and August 1970). I highly recommend this series of articles—they make for challenging reading. For a more complete treatment of his ideas see *Crisis in the Classroom* (New York: Random House, 1970).

[9]See, for example: Sandra S. Davis, "The Pied Piper Way to Reading," *High Points* (Winter 1968), p. 8; Martha Fusshippel, "History in Dramatics," *Instructor* (February 1968), pp. 124–126; Wanna M. Zinsmaster, "Contributions of Creative Dramatics to the Teaching of Social Studies," *Speech Teacher* (November 1965), pp. 205–213.

All of these are taken to be frills, indulged in as long as expenditures are minimal, but eliminated at the first signs of waning budgets. People responsible for planning programs add such subjects when convenient and eliminate them when it appears financially necessary.

Yet another reason for this minimal impact of drama may be the experiences children typically undergo in drama. Most of these are long on such factors as creativity and self-expression, but short on the structure or sequence which allows for growth. In far too many cases, any growth in drama skills may be attributed to simple maturity or individual talent, rather than to the efficiency of the program. Indeed, one classroom teacher—not a theoretician—has recently made a very persuasive statement of the need for a structured program which will teach the specific skills necessary to successful drama experiences.[10]

Oster tried drama with her children, perhaps as you have tried, and she was disappointed with the results. Because she could not find the help she wanted from authorities in the field, she worked to pinpoint a sequence of specific drama skills to teach children. These skills range from simple pantomime of common activities, like picking up a fork, to more elaborate techniques for faking physical conflict. After identifying these skills, Oster taught them in a systematic fashion to provide a repertoire of skills which children could use when they were appropriate. The article makes encouraging reading for a classroom teacher whose experiences with drama have been less rewarding than desired.

In addition to this attempt at outlining more specifically a sequence of steps which may ensure success with drama, another current idea in education—behavioral objectives—has also been applied to creative drama. In a recent, interesting attempt, Shaw has specified with meticulous care the behavioral objectives which should be part of a drama program.[11] Although too recent to as yet have had much impact, we can hope that both these new attempts to clearly identify the sequence and objectives of drama may result in increased vigor for the programs.

Given the current minimal importance of drama, I would like to suggest another method by which such programs may be justified to doubting parents, supervisors, and principals. That is by exploring more fully the ways in which drama can be seen as an integral part of the language arts program and as a means of teaching about many facets of these arts in an exciting fashion. Drama can easily be an avenue to more effective teaching of the language arts and, thus, one can justify making it an integral part of an elementary curriculum.

---

[10]Gwen Oster, "Structure in Creativity," *Elementary English* (April 1969), pp. 438–443.

[11]Ann Shaw, *A Taxonomy of Objectives in Creative Dramatics* (New York: Columbia University, unpublished Ph.D. dissertation, 1968).

Drama and the Reading Program

As was pointed out in Chapter 1, it is most logical to begin by discussing how drama enriches the reading program, because it is within this context that many teachers begin, by doing simple story dramatizations with children. While it is true this is only one facet of spontaneous drama, it is an easily accessible one and is, therefore, recommended to teachers who have never tried drama.

Spontaneous drama adds interest and vitality to a reading program, no matter which method of teaching is employed. While it is true that some of the first stories in basal readers are ill-suited to dramatization, once one gets beyond such fundamentals, many stories which children will encounter are well-suited to dramatization. Whether this is something like a folk or fairy tale in a basal reader, a tradebook a child might use in an individualized reading program, or a story made up in an experience approach program, many such stories can be dramatized. In thinking about dramatizing stories, it is crucial to make a distinction between two ideas and the terms which describe them. The two terms are *interpretation* and *improvisation*. Though this distinction was made in Chapter 1, it will be repeated here.

In doing story dramatization with children, one begins with *interpretation* of the story, i.e., the teacher encourages children to choose characters in the story and to portray, or act out, the characters' role. In interpreting a story, the emphasis is on fidelity to the author's story line and on retaining the basic characterization. Naturally, each child's individuality will be apparent. If we have five different children who interpret the beast in *Beauty and the Beast*,[12] each will be different. Nevertheless, in interpretation, the emphasis is not on what the child can create, but on his ability to bring to life the author's words.

In doing a story *improvisation,* one uses the basic story as a departure point and asks children questions which will encourage them to extend, expand, or in other ways go beyond the basic thematic material. Children may be encouraged to extend the plot forward or backward in time (Diagram 1, p. 81), or to expand the story, perhaps by adding a character (Diagram 2, p. 82) or enlarging the role played by one already in the story. To take a well-known example, let us consider the vain sisters in Cinderella. Have you ever thought much about them? Probably not. Yet we might gain new insights into their characters as a result of considering such questions as:

---

[12]To motivate this you might use the picture in *The Fairy Tale Book,* translated by Marie Ponsot (New York: The Golden Press, 1958), pp. 96–99. Children enjoy the wide-eyed innocence of Beauty as she comforts the ugly beast. The extensive detail in her costume and the elaborateness of her headdress in the illustration by Adrienne Segur clearly establishes the far-off time and place of the story.

1. What things might have made them the way they were? Had they always acted that way? If not, when and why did their personalities change?
2. In what ways were they different? (The story portrays them in silhouette, without much detail.) Are there differences about them we can infer from the story?
3. Were they interested in anything beyond their finery? Had they any talents? What things might they have been good at doing? Did they have any friends? Who could have been interested in such selfish sisters? What evidence is there to support any interpretation?
4. What might have happened if Cinderella's mother had not died? What could have happened if one of the sister's feet had fit the slipper? Or if the prince had dropped it on the marble floor of the palace, and it had shattered?

These are specific questions about only two characters. There are some more general questions which the leader keeps in mind as he encourages children to probe into characters in an effort to make them come to life. The physical, social and psychological facets of the characters need to be considered. In discussing *physical aspects* we are concerned with such questions as:

1. What age do we think the character might be? What evidence do we have about this?
2. What is the character's health condition? An exuberant child will move differently than would Princess Lenore when she was ill.[13]
3. What is the appearance of the character? Obviously Mr. Toad[14] would move very differently than would Puss in *Puss in Boots*.[15]

Related to *social aspects* of the character, we help children to think about such questions as:

---

[13]James Thurber, *Many Moons* (See annotation in Chapter 5, p. 000).

[14]The adventures of the irrepressible Mr. Toad in Kenneth Grahame *The Wind in the Willows* (New York: Charles Scribner's Sons, 1953) make good material for improvisations. Stoic mole and acceptant Ratty make good character contrasts, and the drawings evoke a pastoral time and place very unlike our own.

[15]You might use Charles Perrault, *Puss in Boots* (New York: Charles Scribner's Sons, 1952) for motivation. The illustrations by Marcia Brown depict the debonaire cat attired in his swashbuckling clothes. The story offers a wide variety of people from the ogre to the princess.

DIAGRAM 1

Plot Extension Based on a Story[*]

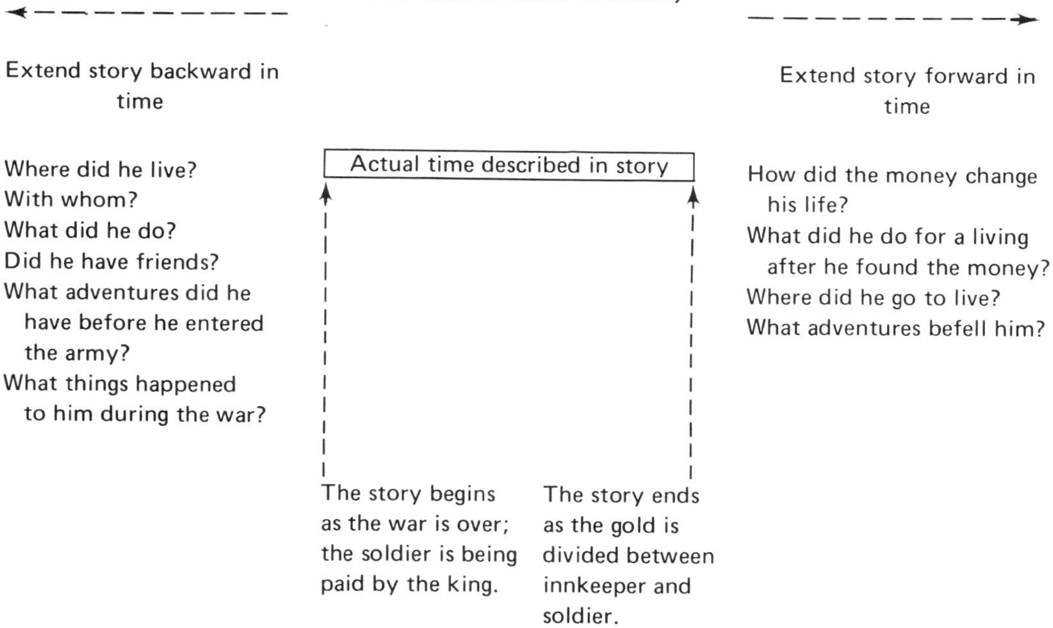

Extend story backward in time ←- - - - - -

Extend story forward in time - - - - - - →

| Actual time described in story |

Where did he live?
With whom?
What did he do?
Did he have friends?
What adventures did he have before he entered the army?
What things happened to him during the war?

The story begins as the war is over; the soldier is being paid by the king.

The story ends as the gold is divided between innkeeper and soldier.

How did the money change his life?
What did he do for a living after he found the money?
Where did he go to live?
What adventures befell him?

---

[*] Based on the story "The Knapsack" in Virginia Haviland, *Favorite Fairy Tales Told in Denmark* (Boston: Little, Brown and Co., 1971).

82   Drama As A Language Art

DIAGRAM 2

*Character Expansion Based on a Story**

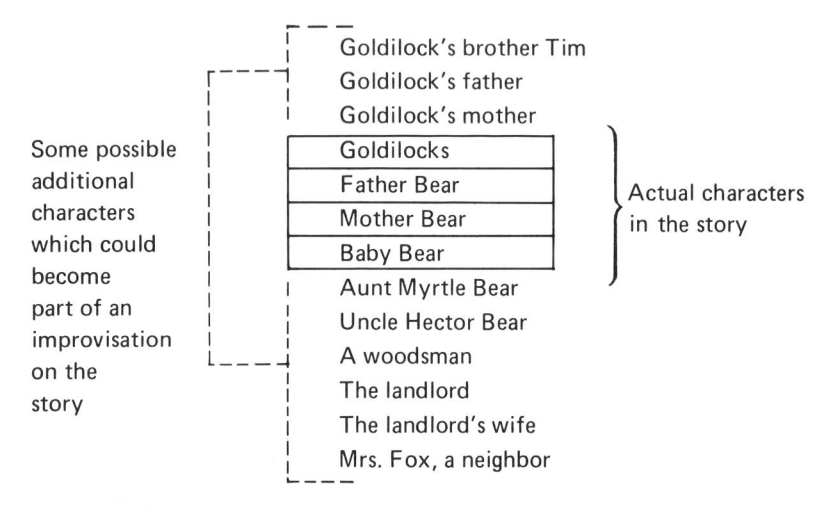

```
                              Goldilock's brother Tim
                              Goldilock's father
                              Goldilock's mother
Some possible                 ┌─────────────────┐
additional                    │ Goldilocks      │
characters                    │ Father Bear     │  } Actual characters
which could                   │ Mother Bear     │    in the story
become                        │ Baby Bear       │
part of an                    └─────────────────┘
improvisation                 Aunt Myrtle Bear
on the                        Uncle Hector Bear
story                         A woodsman
                              The landlord
                              The landlord's wife
                              Mrs. Fox, a neighbor
```

1. What occupation does the character pursue? What effects might that have on him?
2. What kind of home life does the character have? How does he relate to others in his home? (Stories by Elizabeth Enright and Lois Lenski are particularly good ones to use when exploring family relationships.)
3. What kind of personal relationships does the character have outside the family? What clues do these relationships give us about the nature of the character?

Related to *psychological aspects* of the character, we may encourage children to think of the following questions:

1. What do we know, or what can we infer, about the *feelings* of the character? Do we see shifts in the feelings of the character as the story progresses? How are these shifts manifested in behaviors?
2. What do the character's actions and words tell us about his attitudes? Do we see changes in these as the story progresses? If we are improvising, can we infer how the character might feel, or what his attitudes might be in situations other than those described in the story?

---

*Based on the story, "The Three Bears." Children enjoy the illustrations for this story included in *The Arthur Rockham Fairy Book,* pp. 200–205. (Philadelphia: J. B. Lippincott, n.d.).

By judicious use of questions about any basic story, the teacher can lead children from simple *interpretation* into *improvisation* based upon the story. In a recent session with college juniors preparing to do spontaneous drama with children, we explored this question-asking ability. Students came up with the following suggestions about favorite stories.

Cinderella

1. What changes might have occurred if Cinderella had a Fairy Godfather instead of a Fairy Godmother?
2. How could the prince have found Cinderella if the glass slipper shattered on the steps?
3. What if Cinderella had stepbrothers instead of stepsisters?
4. What would have happened if Cinderella had broken her foot?

Little Red Riding Hood[16]

1. What might have happened if the man hadn't come to kill the wolf at the end of the story?
2. What might have happened if Grandma had realized that the wolf was at the door and she hadn't let him in?

Little Miss Muffett

1. What could have happened if she had liked spiders?

Goldilocks and the Three Bears

1. What could have happened if Goldilocks had decided to stay in the forest with the bears?
2. Suppose the porridge had been the right temperature and the bears did not have to go for a walk—what might have happened then?

Snow White and the Seven Dwarfs

1. How could the queen have found out about Snow White if she had no magic mirror?
2. Who might have taken in Snow White, if the dwarfs had not?
3. How would the other dwarfs have acted if Snow White had married one of them?
4. What would have happened if someone would have kissed Snow White before the Prince did, e.g., a beggar?

---

[16] There are innumerable versions of this story. You might use the one with illustrations by Bernadette (Cleveland: World Publishing Company, 1968), which features a very demure Little Red depicted in luscious full color which is almost sensuous. Or, you might try using the version with pictures by Harriet Pincus (New York: Harcourt Brace Jovanovich, 1968) which features a very plain, almost dumpy looking Little Red, who contrasts with the brave woodsman, dashingly adorned in a checkered cap.

Jack and the Beanstalk

1. What if a beautiful princess had lived at the top of the beanstalk instead of a giant?
2. What if Jack wasn't able to chop the beanstalk down in time?
3. What would Jack have done if the beanstalk had wilted after he reached the cloud where the giant lived?

Midas Touch

1. What if King Midas had touched his head and turned himself to gold?
2. What would have happened if the man told Midas that he would no longer have the golden touch, but that he couldn't reverse those things which were already gold, including his daughter?

Hansel and Gretel

1. What would have happened if the house had been made of squash and spinach?
2. What would have happened if the witch had planned to starve them instead of push them into the oven?
3. What would have happened if the bread crumbs had not been eaten by the birds?

Take a story with which you are familiar and try this approach. You'll be surprised at the possibilities which will become apparent as you think about it.

If the teacher is able to lead children through interpreting stories to improvising on stories, such activities will greatly enrich the reading program. Related to the reading program is the literature program, the scope of which is broadened when drama becomes an integral part of the language arts curriculum.

Drama and the Literature Program

For too long, according to writers on the topic, children's literature has been the neglected stepchild in the language arts curriculum.[17] One easy way to remedy this is to use literature as motivation for improvisation. Though drama leaders never limit themselves only to literature,

---

[17]See, for example, the perceptive, comprehensive, and easy-to-read report on the subject by Norine Odland, *Teaching Literature in the Elementary School* (Champaign: National Council of Teachers of English, 1969).

knowing that movement and sensory motivations are important, using poetry and prose for this purpose ensures exposure to a larger quantity of literature than children ordinarily encounter. Many of the pieces the teacher reads to his children during the fifteen or twenty minutes each day which make up the literature program can provide departure points for drama.

Probably there are few of us, as adults, who feel that, as children, our exposure to poetry was as rich, varied, and pleasant as it could have been. Probably there are still fewer of us, as teachers, who feel we are providing children with an exposure to poetry as stimulating, diversified, and challenging as we would like. One way to do this is to make more use of poetry in drama sessions. As we read widely, we find many poems of use. The most important quality in poetry is that of *action*. As you read, search for verbs appropriate for acting out. Thus, we find that children can:

>wiggle[18]
>
>a-scampering[19]
>
>go bounding[20]
>
>glibly slither[21]
>
>trudge[22]
>
>creep[23]
>
>flash[24]
>
>tripping[25]

We also broaden children's exposure to prose by using stories (or parts of them) as motivation for improvisation. You might try using the charming story of winsome Princess Lenore and her illness resulting from a surfeit of raspberry tarts.[26] Or as a contrast, try using episodes from the life of brash *Harriet the Spy*,[27] whom children find to be a delightful terror.

---

[18]Monica Shannon, "Only My Opinion," in *Arbuthnot Anthology of Children's Literature*, ed. May Hill Arbuthnot, op. cit., p. 118.
[19]Walter de la Mare, "The Ship of Rio," ibid., p. 120.
[20]Kenyon Cox, "The Kangarooster," ibid., p. 121.
[21]Palmer Brown, "The Spangled Pandemonium," ibid., p. 123.
[22]Henrich Hoffman, "The Story of Johnny Head-In-Air," ibid., p. 128.
[23]Florence Page Jaques, "A Goblinade," ibid., p. 142.
[24]Rose Flyeman, "Yesterday in Oxford Street," ibid., p. 137.
[25]Mary Jane Carr, "When a Ring's Around the Moon," ibid., p. 138.
[26]James Thurber, *Many Moons* (New York: Harcourt Brace Jovanovich, 1943).
[27]Louise Fitzhugh, *Harriet the Spy* (New York: Harper & Row, 1964).

Boys will be particularly taken with the endless possibilities offered by the adventures of Milo in *The Phantom Tollbooth*.[28] Younger boys have enjoyed the adventures of Peter, as depicted by Ezra Jack Keats.[29]

In these, as in any stories you use, the *action* is the crucial element. All descriptive passages need to be rather ruthlessly eliminated in an attempt to pare the story down to the basic skeleton of action so that it can be played.*

If you are uncertain about your ability to select and adapt prose appropriate to dramatization, do find a copy of *Stories to Dramatize* by Winifred Ward.[30] It is a standard work concerned with these problems by the woman responsible for introducing drama into the elementary curriculum. In addition to providing stories already adapted for improvising, the book offers many suggestions about how to select and adapt stories yourself.

The stories you use need, of course, to be read in their entirety to children, either before or after their use as motivation for drama. This oral reading during the literature period allows children to savor the descriptive paragraphs which may be lost in the active involvement of improvising.

Oral Language Development

Probably one of the strongest contributions drama makes is to *oral language proficiency*. Many authorities have pointed out the pervasiveness of oral language in adult life, and yet the elementary language arts curriculum is only now beginning to reflect this reality, as it sheds an overemphasis on written language.

There are several facets of oral language facility which drama encourages. The first of these is *spontaneous oral composition*. That is, in drama situations, we very frequently challenge children to create dialogue, to think orally on their feet, or to compose as they go. At times we give them situational clues, specifying where they are, who they are, and what the problem is. For instance, the teacher might divide the children into groups of three and specify:

> You are yourself coming home from school late and encountering your annoyed mother in the kitchen as she makes supper. Your little brother, who thinks it is funny, makes comments.

---

[28]Norton Juster, *The Phantom Tollbooth* (New York: Random House, 1961).

[29]Ezra Jack Keats, *A Letter to Amy* (New York: Harper & Row, 1968), and *Peter's Chair* (New York: Harper & Row, 1967).

[30]Winifred Ward, *Stories to Dramatize* (Anchorage, Ky.: Children's Theatre Press, 1952).

*See Chapter 4, p. 000, for a description of units of action analysis.

Children are then allowed time to create a dialogue resulting from the situation. After some time to work on these, the groups present the spontaneous dialogues for the other children.

At other times, perhaps with older children, we structure the situation less completely. This is what Moffett calls the "minimal situation."[31] We might say:

> Imagine you are a teacher and the other person is somebody's mother. Now, make something happen.

Sometimes, we may structure the situation to an even lesser degree, using a *conflict line* to motivate children. A conflict line is a single line which indicates some unspecified conflict which children may develop in many different ways. Some examples might be:

> I wonder why they're not here yet.
> I couldn't believe Sally really said that.
> That's not what we agreed to do.
> Can you explain to me how this happened?
> Can you see what that is up ahead?

Because conflict lines are so open-ended, and yet do give children some structure on which to build, the same line can be used by several different groups with interesting results. In working with a class of thirty children, the leader might, for example, divide them into six small groups, each working with the same line. Comparing and contrasting the resulting improvisations would reveal wide differences in what the groups had been able to create.

In such situations as these, we help children to work on the ability to create oral dialogue which is not written down and to project themselves into the person they are being, as they act or interact verbally in ways the person might.

Related to oral language proficiency is the conscious understanding of such *paralinguistic* elements as pitch, stress, and juncture, which were discussed in Chapter 2. Sometimes we show children pictures of people and ask that they create voices to go with those people. We think about such questions as:

> How would these people be likely to say a particular sentence?
> How might each of them use pitch, stress, and juncture to convey their ideas?

---

[31] James Moffett, *A Student Centered Language Arts Curriculum* (Boston: Houghton Mifflin, 1968).

88 Drama As A Language Art

In this situation, as in so many others in drama, we are asking children to take a small bit of information and to build upon it.

Sometimes we simply ask children to take a sentence from their improvisation and manipulate it in as many subtle ways as possible. An alert leader will notice sentences in the children's dialogue which lend themselves to multiple interpretation. He will encourage them to try out different ways of using paralanguage elements to change the meaning. For an example, refer to p. 33 in Chapter 2.

We can also help children understand the variety of dialects which are most obviously manifested in oral language, by using stories containing such dialects as departure points in drama. When we use such stories as *Strawberry Girl* by Lenski,[32] *Thee, Hannah* by De Angeli,[33] and *Roosevelt Grady* by Shotwell,[34] we may build both an understanding of and a tolerance for people whose oral speech patterns are unlike our own. This is especially crucial in a time when we are becoming increasingly aware that too many children never encounter someone who speaks a dialect unlike their own. Though we never insist that children use the dialects while playing such a story, if this happens we encourage it as an additional language learning through drama. Mable Henry describes these learnings in the following way:

> Did the character speak as they would have in the situation? Amazingly, children are more aware of speech patterns that indicate class and locale than we imagine, and the search for better words to incorporate into the dialogue sends them to the story itself; vocabulary and word recognition become concomitant gains. Words take on meaning in context and in terms of the child's need for them.[35]

The anecdote which best illustrates her point is about a boy who was portraying King Midas:

> In one group of seven-year-olds, King Midas said, "Ok, y' c'n go." He stopped dead and said aloud, to himself more than to the group, "No, kings don't talk like that." He then resumed his character and said imperiously, "Very well, you are dismissed."[36]

Related to these learnings about voice and words is the challenge drama offers to create sounds with the voice. The challenge of creating

---

[32]Lois Lenski, *Strawberry Girl* (Philadelphia: J. B. Lippincott, 1945).
[33]Marguerite De Angeli, *Thee, Hannah* (Garden City, N.Y.: Doubleday & Co., 1940).
[34]Louisa R. Shotwell, *Roosevelt Grady* (New York: Grossett & Dunlap, 1963).
[35]Mable Wright Henry, ed. *Creative Experiences in Oral Language* (Champaign: National Council of Teachers of English, 1967), pp. 56–57.
[36]Ibid., pp. 6–7.

sounds, for instance when we are using a poem about animals, helps children to understand the beauty they can create and extends the expressive range of their voices. Using Durston's poem "The Hippopotamus,"[37] we encourage children to experiment with the sounds the animal might make. Or, we might use "The Pheasant" by Coffin[38] to explore how the sounds made by the animals could change as the poem moves inexorably to its conclusion.

There are more abstract sounds with which children may experiment. They take delight, for example, in interpreting the less recognizable sounds made by the furies, released when Pandora succumbs to temptation.[39] These are neither human nor animal sounds and are unlike anything we have ever heard before, because they are made by strange creatures outside our experience. As such they provide a definite challenge to children's inventiveness, and the results give them insights into the expressive qualities of their voices.

Nonverbal Elements

Spontaneous drama allows us to discover some elements related to oral language which are too frequently ignored. As children work they can be made aware of the importance of both kinesics and bodily movement as adjuncts of communication.

The psychologist Mehrabian[40] tells us that kinesics account for about 55 percent of the total communicated message. By kinesics we mean those bodily movements made by arms, hands, shoulders, and the myriad subtle facial gestures by which we augment the basic message.

Everyone makes use of these additions to the basic flow of speech sounds, though often our use of them is unconscious. It is only when the discrepancy between oral speech and the kinesics becomes apparent that we pause to notice this phenomenon. Unfortunately, we seldom proceed to the next step, which is the conscious manipulation of these kinesic elements to intensify or augment the words we use.

We challenge children to do this consciously when we ask them to think about, and then to show us, how characters might look, or what kinesics they might use, when in a particular situation. We might find a drama program involving children planning kinesics for the following:

---

[37]Included in Arbuthnot's anthology, op. cit., p. 75.

[38]Ibid., p. 54.

[39]Nathaniel Hawthorne, *Pandora's Box* (New York: McGraw-Hill, 1967), illustrated by Paul Galdone. Few adults know that Hawthorne wrote stories for children, including a version of this myth and one of the *Midas Touch*. The value of his version is that it provides much more detail than does the original myth. The illustrations, done very casually in monochrome color and ink line, evoke the innocence of Pandora.

[40]Albert Mehrabian and Susan R. Ferris, op. cit.

1. Alice, as the bewildering queen takes her arm.
2. The two sisters at the moment the glass slipper slides onto Cinderella's foot.
3. The wolf as he tries to talk his way into grandmother's house.
4. The wicked queen as she offers the apple to Snow White.
5. Dorothy, as she bids goodbye to her friends as she leaves Oz.

A definable difference exists between kinesics and *bodily movement,* the latter characterized as larger movements taking place in the context of the space which is available.

Of recent interest to the general public because of the new and popular book entitled *Body Language* by Julius Fast,[41] this aspect of communication has been for some time a concern of drama people. Indeed, Gladys Andrews wrote convincingly some time ago of the need for children to understand the relationship between their bodies and the space around them. Her book on rhythmic movement, though an older one, still provides valuable insights into this area of concern.[42]

We frequently encourage children to work with movement in spontaneous dramatics to make them aware of how this augments communication. Sometimes we work with animal movement. The poem by Mary Austin entitled "The Sandhill Crane" is an especially good one to use because of its variety of verbs.* The poem speaks of the crane *stalking,* the little frogs *jumping,* the minnows *scuttling,* the chipmunks *stopping,* the gophers *hiding,* and the mice *whispering.*

We talk about these verbs and encourage children to interpret these words in movement. Next, we have them propose other animals which might be suggested by the line in the poem which mentions "field folk," and we add a variety of animals and movements until we have an entire menagerie to challenge our ability.

We also work to interpret body movements of humans. The problem here, as elsewhere in drama, is to have children create without resorting to stereotypes. In her film *Creative Drama: The First Steps* Rita Crist helps children to move beyond the stereotype of a little old woman as having a bent back which impedes her movement. This is the first characteristic which comes to many children's minds, and she tries to help them see that, like people of all ages, old people cannot realistically be stereotyped in one way. She talks with them about other aspects of age and how these are manifested differently in different people.

---

[41]Julius Fast, *Body Language* (New York: M. Evans & Co., 1970).

[42]Gladys Andrews, *Creative Rhythmic Movement for Children* (New York: Prentice-Hall, 1954).

*See Chapter 5, p. 115.

We might use *The Magic Bed-Knob* by Mary Norton,[43] for example, to encourage children to think about the ways body movement differs among people. The story provides some large contrasts—for instance, between the inquisitive young children and the fastidious, middle-aged Miss Price. It also provides some small contrasts (perhaps more difficult to achieve) in the differences in body movements between the three children, all of whom are about the same age. A successful characterization of ebullient Paul, helpful Carey, and bossy Charles would entail some differences in physical movements.

In these three examples, and indeed in many aspects of drama, we are working for *particularization* of ideas. In the example given above, the idea of "field folk" is not specific enough. We need to spell out what kinds of field folk are possible and then also detail the particular information about each one. If rabbit is suggested by a child, we need to pursue what kind of rabbit: old or young, male or female, active or feeble, wild or domestic?

Similarly, the little old woman Crist's film needs to be particularized. Who is she? Is she a cranky old lady or a nice old lady? We can even explore how she *feels* about where she is going. As each child begins to develop his own answers to these questions, the improvisation takes on character and depth.

The particularization of the three children in *The Magic Bed-Knob* requires even more thought, since they are of similar ages and, thus, share certain physical characteristics and movement qualities.

The attempt to have children particularize movement is worthwhile, even though at times the best intentions of the leader may go awry. Once while working with a group of kindergarten children on the idea of different types of movement, it became apparent that I was not getting through to one little girl. We had talked about people movement, especially about how daddies move differently than mommies and brothers than sisters. The little girl was adamant in insisting that in her family everybody walked the same way. A very helpful little boy sitting next to her poked her in the ribs with his elbow and looked at her in a disgusted fashion. "What's the matter," he asked, "ain't you got no crippled sisters at home?" At which time we moved to another activity, despite my conviction that particularization of movement is crucial to drama!

Pantomime

Pantomime, an intergral part of spontaneous drama and a concern of the participants at any level of experience, is related to movement. Being

---

[43]Mary Norton, *The Magic Bed-Knob* (New York: Hyperion Press, 1943). See also Chapter 5, pp. 134–142.

able to communicate through one's body and, thus, being able to avoid the reliance on spoken words of explanation is a skill which is of much value in drama. Such pantomime may be a tiny fragment, perhaps as momentary as unscrewing the top on a salt shaker or lifting a glass to drink. Or it may be an involved sequence of separate pantomimed actions which flow together to tell a story, perhaps of the many actions involved in getting ready for, going to, and returning home from a party.

An important thing to remember about pantomime is that it is a *skill*. Whether one is seeing a kindergarten child pantomiming bouncing a ball, or the master Marceau[44] in an involved story sequence, good pantomime is always the result of both thought and practice. This is the reason why children's pantomime is often so generalized; it communicates poorly or not at all. In order to pantomime well, one must perform a series of steps, the first of which is to *particularize* in the mind the actions and objects which are to be portrayed.

If children are to pantomime opening a box, for example, they must answer some questions in their mind before they begin.

1. How large a box is it?
2. Of what is it made?
3. How does it open?
4. On what is it sitting?
5. What is inside of it?
6. How is it fastened shut?

How the child answers these questions will affect how the hand muscles, the arm muscles, and even the torso muscles move as one performs the pantomime. At first these questions need to be posed by the leader orally, to challenge the group to think about these problems. As children develop more mature drama skills, they will ask the questions of themselves.

In thinking about picking up a fork, children would need to think about such questions as:

1. Who is doing this? A child picks up a fork differently from an aging and arthritic grandfather.
2. Of what material is it made? A plastic fork taken along to a picnic would weigh differently than a heavy silver one used at a banquet.

---

[44]You may find some ideas for pantomime in *The Marcel Marceau Alphabet Book* (Garden City, N.Y.: Doubleday & Co., 1970).

3. For what is it being used? If one is trying to maneuver spaghetti to the mouth, the approach with the fork is considerably different from eating something solid like meat loaf.

In these examples the common denominator has been the mental preparation involved in pantomiming the physical movement. The leader may try to establish this mental set by talking with the children about such aspects of the pantomime as these. Or he may use a different approach and have the children observe themselves closely as they use the real object. For some children, picking up a real pencil helps them by watching how their arm and hand muscles move. Most of the physical actions we make are unconscious ones, and observing reality before attempting to re-create the reality in pantomime may help some children to become better at "miming."

After establishing the action or pantomime mentally, the child needs to practice it physically until he eliminates all actions which are unnecessary and strengthens those which communicate. This practice should vary in many ways:

1. Perform the action slower or faster.
2. Perform it with one hand (or foot) and then the other.
3. Do it closer to the body or farther away.
4. Do it in a large space or a small space.
5. Perform it with your body in a different position, e.g., standing, sitting, lying down.

Later you may want to add other variations, such as doing the movement or action with one other person, with two, or with a small group. No matter what the sequence of practice, the important thing is that children realize that to do successful pantomime, the actions need practice in order to be convincing.

After practicing the pantomime, the children need opportunities to perform it for others, in order to get others' reaction to it. Though drama does not emphasize an audience, the child interested in perfecting this skill can profit from some evaluation by other children.

After the pantomime is performed, the children may guess what it represents. The important thing to remember is that guessing for the sake of guessing is *not* the goal. If children can't guess what action a child was performing, try to identify with the group what parts of the pantomime did convey an idea and at what point did the idea begin to evade the mime and those watching.

It is wisest to choose ideas for mime from among actions with which the children are familiar, such as actions they perform at home or at school. After children have developed some facility in such topics, they can progress to being people other than themselves doing actions other than their experiences.

As children become more adept at mime, the leader can direct them to simple story dramatization which will utilize pantomime. Then the activity moves from a simple, disconnected pantomime to a more elaborate series of mimes strung together to tell a story. No matter how involved the drama experience becomes, it always is based on the skill of pantomime.

Puppets

In both pantomime and movement experiences, as well as in story dramatization and improvisation, a key factor is the physical involvement of the child. Spontaneous drama requires this active physical involvement; this is a major difference between drama experiences and puppetry, which involves the child only minimally. Puppetry will receive only brief mention, because most drama leaders agree that puppets are not really a part of spontaneous dramatics.

There is no denying that puppets can be a useful adjunct to the language arts program. Writers have detailed the psychological safety they provide children who are hesitant in using oral language.[45] Methodical descriptions are available to help teachers in step-by-step production of puppets.[46] It has been pointed out that puppets can make subject matter come alive, and that older children can study the many different types of puppets.[47] Despite this, the unavoidable conclusion is that puppets and drama are two different things. In all types of dramatic activities, the child uses his body (and his voice) to express his ideas. He may be using his body to respond to music, to visual stimuli, or to a story, but in all cases he is communicating physically, in addition to vocally.

---

[45] See for example: Sima Spector, "Teaching with No Strings," *The Grade Teacher* (November 1968), pp. 71–75; R. K. Carlson, "Raising Self-Concepts of Disadvantaged Children Through Puppetry," *Elementary English* (March 1970), pp. 349–355; L. V. Wall, *The Puppet Book*, (Boston: Plays, Inc., 1965), pp. 66–83.

[46] See for example: Barbara Mathews, "Papier-Maché Puppets," *School Arts* (October 1968), p. 27; Dorothy Richter, *Hand Puppets: How to Make and Use Them* (New York: Frederick Fell, 1970); A. R. Philpott, *Modern Puppetry* (Boston: Plays, Inc., 1966).

[47] Many different varieties of puppets have been created in cultures in different parts of the world. A study of these types would be of interest to intermediate age children. See, for example: Eric Jones, "Everyone's a Puppet Maker," *Grade Teacher* (March 1969), pp. 47–49, which details how to create shadow puppets, a type children don't ordinarily encounter; A. R. Philpott, *The Dictionary of Puppetry* (Boston: Plays, Inc., 1969) includes many terms of interest in such a study, and in addition, innumerable photographs of many different types of puppets.

But, puppets have to be seen as a valid art form, just unrelated. This is not to discourage the teacher from using puppetry, but simply to point out the necessity of viewing the two as quite distinct forms of communication. Though they are quite different, in one way drama and puppetry are similar—both are effective in developing the child's speaking vocabulary.

Vocabulary Development

There are basically two types of vocabulary which can be developed by experiences in drama. The first of these is vocabulary *intrinsic to the art of drama,* which is simply drama terms. The leader does not attempt to consciously teach these terms in an academic way, but rather uses them whenever appropriate because such terms say what he has to say more effectively. Thus, children are exposed to such terms as *sincerity* (used by Crist to mean an honest and consistent response to the motivation), which some leaders refer to as "staying in character." The opposite term is *break,* used when a child loses his concentration and steps out of character. Leaders regularly use such terms as *environment* and *symbol*—even with young children—and children themselves talk about *plot, climax,* and *characterization.*

In one creative drama session I observed recently, first, second, and third grade children were working with the story, "The Brave White Bear of the North." In improvising on this tale, it is essential that children understand the bear as a *symbol* of snow. In this session children used the word *ferocious* to describe the bear and *distracting* to describe the bird's actions. In the same session the leader talked of the father in the story *fashioning* some shelter and the bear *representing* something.

There is also the vocabulary intrinsic to the motivation being used. Much poetry is full of evocative words; these motivate children to movement and action and can, in addition, become part of the children's vocabulary. They learn about mud being *sloozy* in "I Know a Place," and about someone being *sedate* in "Pretending."[48] They are exposed to such words as *luminous* in "Little Picture," *burgeoning* in "Fishing Trip," *distracted* in "Kites," and *phantoms* in "Cloud Shadows."[49]

---

[48]These are only two of the many poems useful for drama found in Myra Cohn Livingston, *Whispers and Other Poems* (New York: Harcourt Brace Jovanovich, 1958). The intimate quality of many of the poems proves to be their most unusual quality.

[49]These are from Siddie Joe Johnson, *Feather in My Hand* (New York: Atheneum, 1967). The sensitive line drawings which illustrate the book make it a visual delight.

Prose can also provide a similar enrichment of vocabulary. When children work with the engrossing tales in *A Book of Witches*,[50] they encounter the *clamour* of witches, some *peevish* princes, *braying* donkeys, the *snuffling* daughters, and a *lamenting* king, as they all go through dangers to *procure* the rewards. Similarly, when they work out the action for the unusually fresh stories in *The Owl's Nest*,[51] they deal with such words as splendor, cunning, grope, stalwart, and ashen.

However, there is a principle we remember—we do not teach these words in any kind of structured, organized way throughout the drama session. Rather we work with the materials in which the words occur, only discussing the words informally, using them to pique children's interest and to broaden their exposure to the wonderful legacy of vocabulary which is theirs. Teachers may elect to do some conscious teaching of these words, but this is always done in periods separate from the drama session.

We sometimes find children making up vocabulary, creating their own *nonce* words.* Henry mentions children using *glusterous* and *lumining* to describe the crystal city in the poem "Behind the Waterfall."[52] These are perfectly acceptable coinages, and by approving them the teacher encourages word play and fosters the idea that language is a changing vehicle for our thoughts.

Development of Listening Skills

Another language skill which may be developed through creative dramatics is listening; there are two types which drama may encourage. The first can be called *basic listening,* which is defined as listening required for the action of the session to continue. That is, children must attend to what is going on in order to say or do whatever comes next. Such listening is necessary in any kind of dramatic activity, whether the child is listening to music in order to respond rhythmically or doing an interpretation of a folk tale.

Basic listening is simple listening for cues, necessary whether one is considering first graders working out the adventures of the Gruff family in *The Three Billy Goats Gruff,* or sixth graders working out

---

[50]Ruth Manning-Sanders, *A Book of Witches* (New York: E. P. Dutton & Co., 1966).

[51]Dorothy Gladys Spicer, *The Owl's Nest* (New York: Coward-McCann, 1968). These distinctive stories, from the northernmost province in the Netherlands, provide a valuable source of drama material.

[52]Winifred Wells, "Behind the Waterfall," in Arbuthnot's anthology, op. cit., p. 149.

*A nonce word is one made and used for one particular occasion, but not adopted into general use.

sequence in *The Adventures of Tom Sawyer*.[53] The cue may be to some action or to words, but children must be actively engaged in listening in order for the session to continue. It is especially necessary when the group is improvising, as the participants often do not know exactly where the improvisation is going.

The second type may be called *evaluative listening,* in which a child listens to the verbal interaction taking place in an attempt to evaluate its effectiveness and his own ideas about how he might do the same dialogue *more* effectively. Frequently, the teacher divides his group in order to provide a chance for every child to participate. For example, when we use the story *Tom Tit Tot,*[54] we are working with four characters. In order to involve every child, the teacher may divide his class into groups of four and allow each group to work out its version of one of the episodes in the story. After children have had the chance to practice their version, they take turns sharing it with the rest of the group. The teacher sets the stage for evaluative listening by discussing with the children the need to listen carefully, by pointing out some special things to listen for, and by reminding them that they will have a chance to discuss what they hear after the playing is over. After the playing, the leader gathers children together to discuss how the segment went. He asks them such questions as:

1. What was particularly effective about the voice of the small little black thing?
2. How could you tell when he was in different moods? When he was teasing the daughter? When he was angry because she guessed his name?
3. Are there ways *you* could use *your* voice to make the small little black thing sound differently?

Children are then encouraged to work out variations, to experiment with doing the voice in ways they feel would be effective. Sometimes the leader may simply try having the children remain seated as they experiment with the voices in the story, instead of playing out the scene physically. However he does it, its effectiveness depends on the children's *evaluative listening.*

---

[53]The leader can decide if he likes the illustrations by David McKay (New York: Grosset & Dunlap, 1946) or those by Norman Rockwell (New York: The Heritage Illustrated Bookshelf, 1940). Either of these is effective in establishing the mood of the small river town. You could use both and encourage children to discuss which of the illustrations they like best and why.

[54]Evaline Ness, illustrator. *Tom Tit Tot* (New York: Charles Scribner's Sons, 1965).

Spontaneous Drama and Creative Writing

Drama can both *lead to* and *come from* creative writing. In either case, both the writing and the dramatizing benefit. We will first consider how drama can lead to creative writing. A leader may motivate children to improvise on an idea, a story, or a picture. As part of the motivation, he explains that at the close of the experience they will write down what has happened. With younger children this may be a simple recording of plot sequence, while with older children it may include a more sophisticated description of such ephemeral elements as tones of voice and facial expressions. After children have done this—rather directly with no emphasis on mechanics—a profitable discussion can ensue about differences between what individual children have written.

This is a good point at which to discuss discrepancies existing among observers' reports of a single event. It is also logical then to discuss the difference between writing basic description and writing about elusive aspects of an improvisation. Describing simple sequences, as what happened first, next, and last, is obviously an easier task than describing the mood of a scene or the feeling of a character. Such discussions lead logically, especially with older children, into considerations of the differences between the written skeletal outline of a play and the physical manifestation of this outline when it is brought to life by the actor's interpretations of the basic directions. While one is not working in spontaneous drama toward formal play making as a goal, such discussions nonetheless give children insights into the theatre and stimulate them to ask questions about aspects of drama not ordinarily considered.

After giving children a chance to discuss such ideas as these, the leader might—in another session—want to reverse direction and have children *interpret* these various written accounts concerning the original improvisation. After providing time for children to write down what they observed in an improvisation, the teacher might select several of the most divergent accounts, then divide the children into groups to play out these written accounts. Differences which became apparent could be discussed. The approach doesn't matter—the point is the rich variety available when working with writing down what is observed.

Drama can also *come from* creative writing. The teacher, using whatever means which seems to work especially well for him, may motivate children to write a story. After this is done, he can select three or four of these stories for use in the spontaneous drama session. Invariably, children will want to know why their story was not chosen, which can lead to a discussion of the characteristics of good motivation for drama. Instead of telling the children what these are, the leader more frequently tries to draw these characteristics from the children. He does so by having them examine the stories which were used, to see which features they have in common. If they were good motivations for drama, they will invariably share some of the following characteristics which make stories effective for playing:

1. Clearly defined, active characters, with whom children can identify.
2. A logical form with an arresting beginning.
3. A clear and uncluttered story line.
4. A climax and a satisfying conclusion.

It is naturally much more effective if children can discover these characteristics by comparing stories, than if they are simply told to them as fact by the leader.

Usually such examination and discussion of stories leads to another request: "Can I rewrite my story so we can use it?" The rewrite sessions which follow, as the teacher helps children to edit characterization, plot, and dialogue, can be very helpful—not only in producing more story motivations for drama, but also in encouraging children to write stories of more intrinsic value as creative writing. The rewriting sessions on a particular story go on for as long as the teacher deems it profitable. Not every story comes to the stage of being usable for dramatization, nor should it. But, because the teacher uses this procedure with children at regular intervals, the children know that if their story is not chosen one time, perhaps it will be chosen another time. This gives them the needed incentive to continue working and refining their skills of writing and dramatizing. These two skills interrelate very easily, and an enrichment of each activity results.

Summary

It seems possible to justify the inclusion of spontaneous drama as an integral part of an elementary curriculum, if one is aware of the way it leads to knowledge about language and the development of language skills. A teacher interested in doing drama with children should be able to convince parents, supervisors, and principals of the validity of drama if he emphasizes the contribution drama makes to the language arts curriculum. Drama can provide an approach to and enrich the learning in the reading program, the literature program, and the areas of oral language development, nonverbal communication, vocabulary development, listening skills, and creative writing. The teacher interested in the benefits drama provides knows his children will grow even in ways other than these, but he may find it easier to proselytize for drama if he emphasizes the richness it adds to the language arts.

5

A Suggested Sequence of Spontaneous Dramatics

Children are enviably succinct in evaluating. A teacher once recommended a book on dinosaurs to a fifth-grade child and was chagrined when he asked the boy how he liked it and his response was, "It told me more than I wanted to know about dinosaurs."

Having read through the first four chapters, perhaps you are feeling much the same—that you already know more about spontaneous drama than you wanted to know. Though the first four chapters are crucial, one more is equally essential. The first four attempted to deal with theoretical concerns: *what* drama is, *how* it is done, and *why* it is one of the language arts.

This chapter attempts to take the ideas presented earlier and to use them as a foundation upon which to build a sequential series of actual experiences with children in an attempt to demonstrate how a leader might plan drama activities. However, the chapter must be seen as an explanation of a *process,* not as a finished *product.* There are probably many ideas included here which you could use, but the more desirable outcome of this chapter is that you see how what has gone before can be used as a basis on which to build a sequence of your own.

What Is a Departure Point?

The materials in this chapter are arranged in ten segments, which are called *departure points.* These are, in essence, suggested ways in which a teacher might begin sessions in spontaneous dramatics.

The materials are called departure points in order to emphasize their expandable nature. Undoubtedly, the materials *should* be used to stimulate many more than ten sessions. The teacher should use his judgement about when to expand, when to contract, and when to terminate the ideas which are included. Thus, the plans are designed to represent an ideal progression of increasingly more complex dramatic experiences, rather than ten actual sessions to be shared in the consecutive order presented here.

BRIEF SUMMARY OF SEQUENCE

Departure Point	Main Emphasis	Motivation
One	Introduction to spontaneous dramatics, Interpretative movement	Words about animal movement
Two	Interpretative movement Simple characterization	Story: Three Billy Goats Gruff—picture: the troll
Three	Abstract movement	Music—fingerpaintings
Four	Interpretative movement Some attention to mood	Poem: The Sandhill Crane
Five	Mood interpretation	Pictures
Six	Characterization Some plot development	Fairy tale: Mrs. Tubbs
Seven	Characterization Plot Incidental dialogue	Story line created by children in response to picture
Eight	Characterization Plot, dialogue, Mood	Mask pictures
Nine	Same as number eight	Story line created by children in response to picture
Ten	Elaboration of two previous sessions	Story: Miss Price

A Suggested Sequence of Spontaneous Dramatics   103

You might have noticed that there is no session motivation specifically devoted to conflict* as a dramatic element as there are to the other commonly identified elements, e.g., mood and character. Rather, conflict forms an integral part of most motivations.

These plans lead from simple to more complex activities. Basically, the program is designed to be done as a sequence; however, the materials chosen, with adaptation, could be used at other places. Because this activity is seen as a part of the language arts program, the lesson material will be flexible enough to respond to children's interests and the demands of the language arts curriculum. For instance, should the children become interested in fairy tales early in the year, the story of Miss Price (session ten) could be used and done differently from the way presented in the plan.

Each of the plans includes several sections:

1. *Group Goals.* These are the purposes of the particular session, that is, what the session is supposed to help children to learn to do. They are not necessarily related to the dramatic understandings the children will be acquiring, but rather are judged to be general "goods" for which the teacher is interested in working.

2. *Drama Goals.* These include the specific drama purposes of the session or the drama abilities which the session is designed to encourage. Frequently, they include a statement of the relation of this particular session to those which preceed or follow it.

3. *Materials.* These include either the actual materials to be used with the children or references to sources of the materials (e.g., a story may be found in several sources).

4. *Method.* This is a brief statement of what the children and teacher might do. Perhaps the largest and most helpful section is the list of questions which the teacher could use to stimulate children to think about the topic and react. These are intended as exemplary, or sample questions; they should be seen simply as stimuli to the teacher, nothing more.

The teacher uses these materials, keeping in mind that the questions are motivations to *action,* not simply to discussion. Though discussion will ensue naturally, the teacher always encourages children to "show," to use their bodies to "become" the animal or person in question, not simply to respond verbally. The intent is to get children up on

---
*This refers to the types of conflict in drama as explained on page 62 in Chapter 3.

their feet interpreting something—*acting*—even if such interpretation is fragmentary.

Departure Point One

Group Goals

1. To introduce children to spontaneous dramatics, through both discussion and rhythmic movement.
2. To further children's skills in group work.
3. To encourage respect for other children's interpretations.

Drama Goals

1. To provide the children with an opportunity to experiment with some simple rhythmic movement by using words about animals to stimulate imaginative interpretation.

Materials

The children probably will have had experience in writing their own stories and in thinking about words—what they can do and the excitement they can add to a story. Since children are accustomed to communicating with words, this is a logical way to introduce them to new experiences. The teacher may use the following list of words (When the children become relaxed, they will be able to add others.):

stalk	slither	clump
hump	stamp	wriggle
slide	glide	bounce
creep	swing	tiptoe
stretch	mince	jump
flit	soar	amble
puddle	arch	slink

Method

1. *Introduction to the idea of spontaneous dramatics.* First the teacher will discuss briefly with the children some of the following:

What is spontaneous dramatics?
Who can do it?

Everyone.

All together?

Sometimes everybody, sometimes just a few—then the rest of us will be audience.

Did someone make it up?

Why should we do it?

So we can learn to say something with our bodies and learn many ways of telling our thoughts—in painting, in writing, in musical notes.

How do we share our thoughts?

We could do it in any of the ways listed above, but another way is dramatics.

How?

By moving—just beautiful movements—by acting out a story, by what we share when we search for an idea.

Do we get a grade for it?

If not, how do we tell if it's good?

We discuss honestly and sincerely.

2. *Introduction to the movement part of the session.* Next the teacher will discuss movement with the children to stimulate them to experiment with movement themselves. The teacher could use a dialogue similiar to the following:

> Now, part of expressing ideas is moving. How do you walk? Do we all walk alike? Show me. Can you go faster? Slower? Have you ever thought about walking before? Probably not—most people don't. (This section may need expanding, especially if the children are quite inhibited. Doing more showing—ways people move, skip, hop, and run—could alleviate this inhibition.)
>
> In what ways do animals move? Differently from us? How? Show me. Have you been to a zoo? Did you see the animals walk while you were there? Do all of them move? All of the time? Sometimes? Which animals hardly move at all? What animals do you know about that you've never seen move?
>
> Of the moving ones, have you ever seen one _____? (At this point, insert one of the words from the list.) Which animal moves like that? Any others? Can you show us a _____ moving like that? Can someone else do it? (Follow the same procedure until all children are involved, then work into using their own words.)

Anticipated Realization of Goals

When this session has been completed several things may have been accomplished:

1. The children in the group may have discovered what spontaneous dramatics is and, more specifically, may have a good idea of interpretation as a part of the art.
2. They may have accepted this activity as a legitimate one to be done in the school room, even though it is quite different from the ones they usually do.
3. The fact that they have done this activity in their classroom in the presence of other children will tend to help release ideas and alleviate inhibition.

Closing Each Session

The teacher should spend some time talking about the following:

1. What we learned new today.
2. What we did new today.
3. Who discovered an especially effective way to show us their idea.
4. What we will do next time (motivation).

Departure Point Two

Group Goals

1. To reinforce the pleasant experience with spontaneous dramatics which the children had the first session.
2. To introduce a new idea—concentrating on one subject.
3. To help children to understand that even though they all work with the same ideas, each person's interpretation of that idea is what is important; therefore, they should respect others' interpretations.
4. To reinforce the necessity to further develop skills of group discussion.

Drama Goals

1. To continue working with movement and, perhaps, some dialogue, *if* the children add it spontaneously. No *emphasis* will be

placed on creation of dialogue, but the ways trolls talk will be mentioned.
2. To reinforce individualization of interpretation.
3. To add a new dimension—visual stimulation.

Materials

1. Story of *The Three Billy Goats Gruff*—this story was chosen because of its familiarity; therefore, it will be easier to approach individualization of movement because of the children's interest. Also, because it is about animals, it repeats the theme of the first session.
2. Pictures of some "trolls."

Method

The teacher should try to relate this to the work done with animals during the previous period. As an example, he could say, "This time we are going to think about a family of animals. They are about to do something interesting, but there is something that tries to stop them."

Next, the leader tells the story. The version in Arbuthnot's anthology (p. 72) is from Sweden. Part of the study of fairy tales during the year will involve finding different versions of the same tale and helping children compare them. While fairy tales with the same subject may be essentially the same in characterization and plot, they often include variation in detail, which is interesting. See, for example, the version of this tale in Huber (p. 249), and also P.C. Asbjornsen, *The Three Billy Goats Gruff* (New York: Harcourt, 1957). This comparing of variety in fairy tales stimulates the children's interest, and thus this fairy tale should be well received when used in the spontaneous dramatics section of the language arts program.

Then the leader moves into a discussion of the story, such as the following:

> Now, we could have an interesting time acting out the story. (The teacher may decide to do this if it seems appropriate. Strictly speaking, acting out the story would be *interpretation* rather than *improvisation,* but for a particular group of children it may be the best way to begin.) But for a moment let's talk about only one person in the story. Not the littlest goat, or the middle goat, or the largest goat. You guessed it—the troll!
>
> What things does the story tell us about the troll? Do we know where he lives? Alone? Had he always lived there? Why might he

have chosen to live there? What kind of a troll do you think he was? Happy? Sad? Ferocious?

Now, could you *be* that troll? What do you suppose he looked like? How might he have moved? Was he graceful? Could he move fast? Ever? How about when he was after a tender young goat?

Show me how you think this troll moved. Where could he go? Did he have any friends? Who? Did he have a family? If he had a family, why don't you all be that family? Mrs. Troll? How was she different? (Let children get up and move like trolls. Compliment children on the variety of interpretations.)

Good! Now let's think about other kinds of trolls. Do you think they all look alike? How could they look different from the one in the story? Would they live in different places? In the woods? In streams of water? At the bottom of lakes? In dark places? Underneath large rocks? In abandoned barns? In hollow trees? How might the woods trolls look, act, behave, move, and walk differently than the lake or stream trolls? Who would like to be one of these other kinds of trolls? Are trolls like anything else you know? Like fairies or elves? How are they different? Do they ever do the same kinds of things? Why do trolls want to be unpleasant? Are there ever any who don't want to be? Are the fairies ever frightened of the trolls?

Do trolls have any enemies? Other than big goats? Who else, besides you, would not like trolls? What things do trolls eat? How do they get their food? Do they raise any of it, or do they just eat people and animals? What kinds of things are in their houses? Do they wear clothes? Where might they get them? What do they do when they are not eating things?

(All of these could be possible departure points for children to begin a simple improvisation-movement activity on trolls. Continue this type of questioning only until the children are motivated.)

All of you are very different from one another. We have talked about this before. So all of your trolls should be different from one another. Some could be tall and thin, others short and stout, still others bent over and withered. What other ways could they look or feel? Show us your kind of troll. Can we tell everything about your troll by just looking? How can we see inside you, to what your ideas about your troll are? (Here reinforce the idea that one must act out one's feelings to communicate them.)

If there is some child who cannot imagine what a troll would be like, the teacher could encourage him to act out a fairy or an elf, as these had been mentioned earlier and are more familiar to a child. It is entirely

A Suggested Sequence of Spontaneous Dramatics 109

possible that some children could not identify with a troll, and no attempt is made to enforce a single idea.

This session includes two ideas for motivation, the pictures and the story, but no attempt has been made as yet to suggest how or when to use the pictures. The teacher may use the pictures as a motivation for group discussion prior to playing out the story. He would encourage the children to discuss what they see in the pictures. If he uses several different pictures illustrating the same story, he would encourage children to discuss similarities and differences. Depending on how well the children responded without them, the teacher might decide to not use them at all, or to postpone using them until a later date and in another context.

Many picture materials that could accompany this story are older and out of print, but undoubtedly are still available in public and school library collections. Following is a list of books containing pictures of trolls which can be used to heighten the stimulus of the session. Out-of-print materials are marked with an asterisk, but are included because they frequently are still available. In all cases, the materials listed are only suggestions, and the individual teacher, being familiar with the resources in his local area, can make substitutions of more appropriate visual motivational material.

1. Blair, Susan, ill.
   Asbjornsen, P. C., ed.
   The Three Billy Goats Gruff
   (New York: Holt, Rinehart & Winston, 1963).*

2. Brown, Marcia, ill.
   Asbjornsen, P. C., and J. E. Moe, eds.
   The Three Billy Goats Gruff
   (New York: Harcourt Brace Jovanovich, 1957).

3. Collin, Hedvig, ill.
   Asbjornsen, P. C., ed.
   East of the Sun and West of the Moon
   (New York: MacMillan, 1953), p. 17.

4. d'Aulaire, Ingri and Edgar Parin, ills. and eds.
   East of the Sun and West of the Moon
   (New York: The Viking Press, 1969), p. 178.

5. Hauman, George and Doris Piper Watty, eds.
   Stories That Never Grow Old
   (New York: Platt & Munk, 1938), p. 59–62.

6. Remington, Barbara, ill.
   Nestrick, Nova, ed.
   The Three Billy Goats Gruff
   (New York: Platt & Munk, 1962).

7. Vroman, Tom, ill.
Asbjornsen, P. C., and J. E. Moe, eds.
East of the Sun and West of the Moon
(New York: Macmillan, 1963), p. 16.

This fairy tale also offers some interesting material for further discussion during the regular language arts period:

1. The particular meaning of the word *burn* is probably foreign to the children. It is chiefly Scottish and dialectical, signifying a brook (see also *bourn*—Anglo-Saxon). In addition to thinking about this unusual word, the teacher could use this as an occasion to talk about words peculiar to certain languages or places and about how words change over time.

2. The word *scarce* in the context of this story is unusual and probably unfamiliar to children. The teacher could call this to the children's attention and pursue samples of words they know that are used in unusual ways.

3. There are nonsense syllables in the story, e.g., snip, snap, and snout. The teacher and children could think about why authors use nonsense syllables and search for examples of them in literature the children can read.

4. The story contains vocabulary words which are just generally unfamiliar, e.g., *curling-stones*. The teacher, perhaps, could help children to understand what these are by comparing them to the flat grinding stones used by Indians to pulverize corn. If possible, the teacher could borrow a curling stone from a local curling group, so the children could see one.

Anticipated Realization of Goals

1. The children will be able to renew acquaintance with an old familiar story.
2. They will see that only *part* of a story is often enough to stimulate an improvisation.
3. They should be more aware that often we tend to ignore what could be the most interesting part of the story, i.e., in this case, the troll.
4. This lesson should have established enough familiarity and ease in moving, so that the children will be prepared for the next session, which will involve music and a more abstract type of movement.

Departure Point Three

Group Goals

1. To help children to become aware that we can use other means of motivation, e.g., music, and pictures (by themselves), to give us ideas about movement.
2. To begin to deal with more abstract ideas, which makes interpretation correspondingly more difficult.
3. To continue building respect for other people's interpretations.

Drama Goals

1. To provide the children with an opportunity to interpret movement as suggested in music and art.
2. To encourage the freedom to react to a variety of stimuli.

Materials

1. Fingerpaintings
2. Recordings (see list p. 113).

The most effective method of motivating this session is to use fingerpaintings done by the children. A few weeks before the teacher could talk with the art teacher in his school and see if he will help the children. In making the fingerpaintings, the children should be encouraged to experiment primarily with large movements, not with subtle textures. After the paintings are made, the teacher can select the ones he feels best serve the purpose of this departure point.

If there is no art teacher in his school, the leader could use any one of many art education method books for help and ideas. One good example is *Art for Primary Grades* by Dorothy S. McIlvain (New York: Putnam, 1961).

Method

1. *Fingerpaintings.* The teacher might use the following approach in introducing the ideas to children:

> Movement is many things, not just motion with our bodies. Today we are going to *see* some movements by artists and then *hear* some by composers. But, we're also going to relate these movements to our bodies.
>
> We'll begin with these fingerpaintings. If you were going to tell someone about them, what would you say? What words would you

use to tell about them? (Encourage the children to describe the pictures, hopefully drawing out descriptions like the following:)

wide, narrow	many, few
soft, sharp	curved, straight
jagged, smooth	open, closed
simple, complicated	curled-up, swoopy

How can lines, after they have been made, look fast, or slow? What things make them look that way? We can be fast and slow, can't we? Who would show me? (Then work into interpreting some of the foregoing descriptions.)

Who could make a wide movement? A narrow one? Which is harder to make—an open or closed movement? Why? Can you pick one of the paintings you especially like? Does it have more than one idea in it? Can you act out what you see in the painting?

There is the possibility that such a discussion and ensuing interpretation would take a whole period. The children could suggest other kinds of movements found in the pictures. If they respond quite well, the teacher could decide to use the music at a later session.

2. *Music.*[2] The teacher could stimulate interest with the following:

Another way we get ideas about how to move is to listen to music. This is perhaps even more difficult than looking at pictures, since we have to listen carefully and move while we listen because, while we can look at something for a long time, music is over very quickly.

I'm going to play some music for you. Just listen the first time through to get acquainted with it, then see if it suggests some kind of movement.

The music listed on p. 113 is divided into four general categories, with three alternatives for each category. While these are not the only categories, or the only types of movements which the piece might suggest, they will at least initiate the work with music as a stimulus.

The reason for three alternatives is that in getting used to music as a means of inspiration, children's attention shouldn't be taken by the

---

[2] The idea of moving to music is dealt with in Anne and Paul Barlin, *The Art of Learning Through Movement* (Los Angeles: The Ward Ritchie Press, 1971). See Chapter 6, p. 154. You may wish to read what they have to say on this topic before doing this session.

large, bold, and relaxed music:

    organ   Mendelssohn, Felix
                  Sonata #3 in A
                  Vox 14030

    orchestral   Mendelssohn, Felix
                  Symphony #5, in d, finale
                  Mercury 50174

    vocal   De Falla, Manuel*
                  Seven Spanish Folk Songs
                  Angel 35775

quiet, peaceful, and introspective music:

    organ   Bach, J. S.
                  "O Mensch Bewein", and
                  "Ich Ruf'Zu Dir"
                  Deutsch Grammaphon 2-D66, Arc 3025-6

    orchestral   Beethoven, Ludwig von
                  Symphony #7, second movement
                  Comman 11014

    vocal   Same as above

stringy, entended, and thin music:

    organ   Hindemith, Paul
                  Sontata for Organ, second movement
                  Columbia ML 5634

    orchestral   Barber, Samuel
                  Adagio for Strings
                  Vanguard 1095

    vocal   Same as above

short, choppy, and agitated music:

    organ   Dupre, Marcel
                  Variations on a Noel, #4 and #7
                  Mercury 50224

    orchestral   Shostakovich, Dmitri
                  Symphony #5, Op. 46, third movement
                  Victor LM 2866

    vocal   Same as above

---

*This one set provides music in each of the categories listed. Using music by one composer adds further unity to the session. While these pieces are vocal, the fact that they are sung in Spanish keeps the children from being distracted by the words. The pieces come across as pure sound and should be quite useful in stimulating rhythmic movement.

instrument making the music, but rather by the type of music it is. For this reason the teacher should probably use either all instrumental, all organ, or all vocal in any one session. Certainly if the teacher finds these particular recordings unavailable, the school music teacher could suggest other possibilities.

Anticipated Realizations of Goals

By this time the children will have been exposed to rhythmic movement stimulation from three sources: 1) words, 2) a story and pictures, and 3) pictures and music. Movement and the freedom to use their bodies to express ideas should no longer seem strange to them, so they should be ready to move into session four which offers some possibilities for mood and sequence development.

Departure Point Four

Group Goals

1. To gain further experience in expressive movement.
2. To respond to poetry as motivation for spontaneous drama activities.
3. To become more aware of the expressive and alliterative qualities of words used in a poem.

Drama Goals

1. To give everyone a chance to interpret the animals in the poem through movement.
2. To stimulate awareness of mood as an element in dramatics improvisation.
3. Perhaps to work out a simple sequence of events. Such sequence would be no more involved than:

> The animals are happily busy.
> The crane comes; the animals hide.
> The crane leaves; the animals come out again.

It will depend on how successful the children are in capturing the mood of the various animals and the tenseness of the situation if the teacher will decide to go to developing a sequence.

Material

THE SANDHILL CRANE[3]
Mary Austin

Whenever the days are cold and clear
The sandhill crane goes walking
Across the field by the flashing weir
Slowly, solemnly stalking.
The little frogs in the tules hear
And jump for their lives when he comes near,
The minnows scuttle away in fear,
When the sandhill crane goes walking.

The field folk know if he comes that way,
Slowly, solemnly stalking,
There is danger and death in the least delay
When the sandhill crane goes walking.
The chipmunks stop in the midst of their play.
The gophers hide in their holes away
And hush, oh hush, the field mice say,
When the sandhill crane goes walking.

Reasons for Selection

1. The poem is entirely about animals, with which children find it easy to empathize.
2. The wide variety of animals mentioned would offer a chance for many of the children to be different things.
3. The variety of verbs is good: goes walking, stalking, hear, jump, scuttle, stop, hide, say.
4. The poem conveys an element of danger/suspense, another feature popular with children. Also, the poem suggests the little animals are in collusion against the crane (something more powerful than they); this is certainly another concept to which children can relate.
5. The descriptions in the poem are specific enough to make dramatization easy, yet general enough to allow for individual interpretation.
6. The unusual words in the poem are a good chance to build the child's sensitivity to the imagery which words can evoke.

---

[3]Mary Austin, *The Children Sing in the Far West* (Boston: Houghton Mifflin, 1928). This poem is also available in Arbuthnot's anthology, p. 53.

7. The alliteration in the poem makes the rhythmic quality apparent; it is aurally quite pleasant.

To illustrate these reasons more clearly, below is an analysis of the verbs in the poem for acting and the alliterations for rhythmic reading. Verbs are marked with dotted lines, alliterations with connecting lines.

> Whenever the days are cold and clear
> The sandhill crane goes walking
> Across the field by the flashing weir
> Slowly, solemnly stalking.
> The little frogs in the tules hear
> And jump for their lives when he comes near,
> The minnows scuttle away in fear
> When the sandhill crane goes walking.
> The field folk know if he comes that way,
> Slowly, solemnly stalking,
> There is danger and death in the least delay
> When the sandhill crane goes walking.
> The chipmunks stop in the midst of their play,
> The gophers hide in their holes away
> And hush, oh hush, the field mice say,
> When the sandhill crane goes walking.

Method

The teacher can explore various ideas with the children in a manner similar to the following:

What kind of birds do we see in our area? What kinds do you know about that live elsewhere? Have you ever seen a crane? (Perhaps someone will suggest a whooping crane, which might lend itself to discussion.)

Mostly we think that birds are our friends. Are birds always friendly and helpful, or are birds sometimes dangerous? To whom? How? Could you show us how?

Today we have a poem about a bird . . . a dangerous one!

At this point, before reading the poem, the teacher would decide if using a picture would motivate the children further. (See list of picture sources following this section.) The teacher then reads the poem to the children. This should be done in its entirety the first time, not pausing to analyze or respond to it. Thinking of this in light of the language arts program, the poem should be presented *first* as an artistic unit, a literary creation which deserves to be treated as a unit. The teacher should be careful to stress alliteration in the poem, as this is a concept with which children should become familiar.

Next, the leader returns to the unusual words in the poem and discusses them with the children, trying to pull suggestions from them about what these words might mean. Then he helps to clarify the images in the poem by presenting the definitions of the words. For example, a *weir* is a dam in a stream to raise the water level or divert its flow, and *tules* is a large variety of bulrush, which grows abundantly on overflowed land.

The teacher can then continue the discussion:

What kinds of pictures can you see in your mind as you hear the poem? What time of year is it in the poem? Where did the action take place? Who was there? What did they do? What kind of danger was there? From whom? What would you do? What did the others do to escape?

How did the crane come across the field? How is stalking different from just walking? Could you move like a:

crane	chipmunk
frog	gopher
minnow	field mouse
bull frog	mosquito

Who else might be field folk? Can you move like any of them?

A Suggested Sequence of Spontaneous Dramatics

Image Analysis

The poem provides a variety of image stimulus for children:

Sensory: *cold and clear.* Can you feel the kind of day it was? What time of the year might it have been?

Visual: *the flashing weir.* Can you see the glint of the cold sunlight on the water?

Auditory: *hush, oh hush.* The frogs hear the sound of the crane's feet as he moves through the dry rubble of the field. Can you hear him coming? Can you hear the silence descend until the only sound in the field is that of the crane's feet breaking the dried and brittle tules?

Kinesthetic: *scuttle, stalking.* How would it feel to walk across those dried and brittle weeds? Different than walking through the squishy mud? Show us how.

References

Pictures of the sandhill crane can be found in the following:

Audubon, John James, *Birds of America* (New York: Macmillan, 1950), p. 131.

The Audubon Magazine (July 1963), p. 212.

_____. (November 1963), p. 356.

_____. (November 1957), p. 264.

_____. (November 1955), p. 251.

Natural History Magazine (October 1955), p. 420.

Nature Magazine (May 1956), p. 237.

Other materials by Mary Austin include:

Land of Little Rain (Peter Smith, 1961).
One Hundred Miles on Horseback (Dawson's, 1963).

Anticipated Realization of Goals

1. By now children should be aware that spontaneous dramatics can be done with a variety of source materials. To this point sessions have made use of a fairy tale, records, paintings, and now a poem.

2. The children should be developing a sensitivity to poetry. The teacher should be involving children in many correlative activities with poetry, such as 1) reading it in reading class, 2) listening to it in sharing

time, 3) writing it, 4) illustrating other people's poems, and 5) doing choral speaking.

The introduction of poetry could be done at the beginning of the year, and various poems should be shared. About a week before using this poem in spontaneous dramatics, the teacher should begin an intensive unit on poetry to provide a lead into its use here.

3. The leader has reinforced the importance of word choice to the children. Throughout the year the teacher should put much emphasis on vocabulary, to make children aware of the wonder of words and what can be done with them, but not requiring them to memorize specific definitions.

4. The children have had a chance to interpret a more literal stimulus. The approach used in session three, music and fingerpaintings, requires a higher level of abstract conceptualization than any of the other sessions. Depending on its effectiveness with the children, the teacher might or might not pursue it further. That is, should they be able to do that interpretation, he would present more of that type of stimulation. However, if it presents a difficulty to them, he should go directly into this session to give them an easier success and to reinforce their confidence in their ability to do spontaneous dramatics.

Departure Point Five

Group Goals

1. To provide children with material about people for reflection and interpretation.
2. To give them a chance to verbalize, to discuss the picture, and to see again that an idea communicated through one medium can be recommunicated through another.
3. To make them aware of the term *mood.* This is the first of the sessions in which mood is the *major* emphasis. Naturally, this has come up in incidental ways previously—the crane in session four demands a mood interpretation.

Drama Goals

1. To help children to understand that mood is part of *any* dramatic experience.
2. To bring to a conscious level how we communicate mood. This is a difficult concept. We all feel intensely, but to show others how we feel is more difficult.

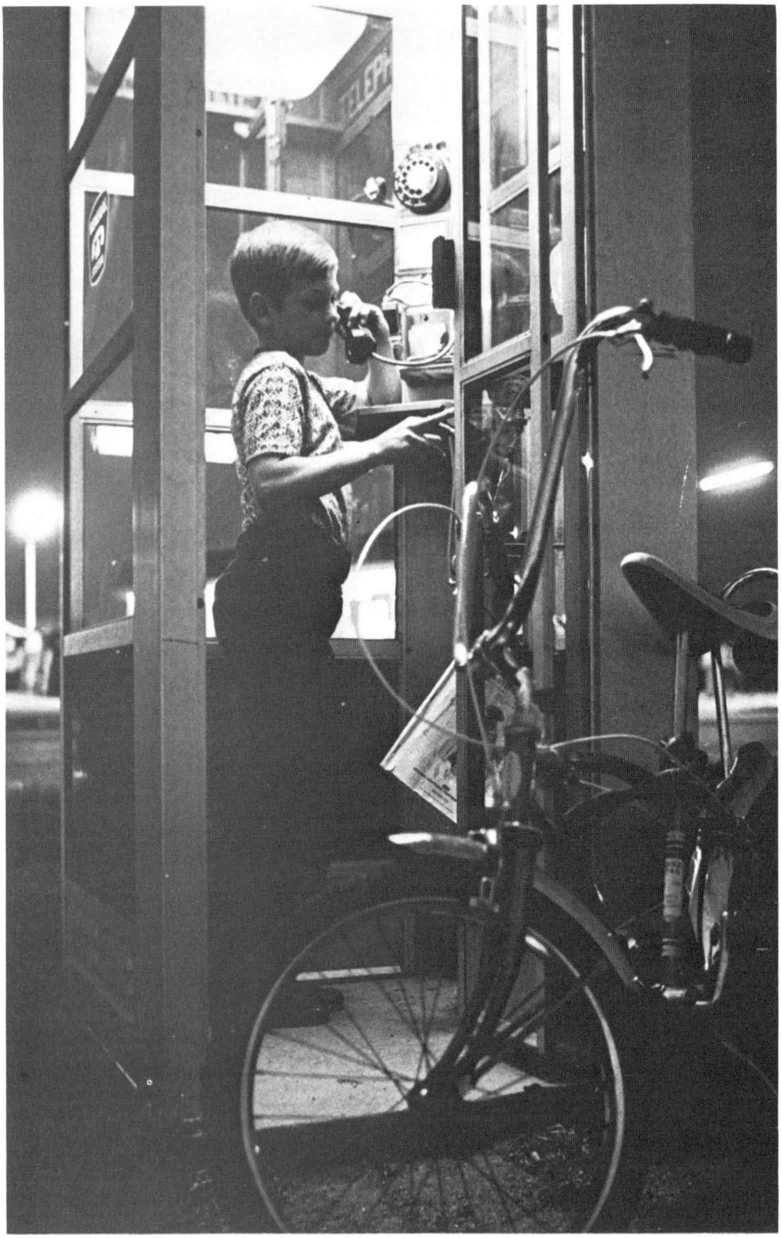

3. To give the children a chance to react to the picture and to interpret the moods; then, to get them to share their interpretations of time they felt in similar or different moods.

Materials

All questions in the following section are keyed to the picture on page 120. (It can be enlarged in an opaque projector if so desired.) However, any other picture in which some unspecified conflict or danger is suggested, rather than implicitly shown, can be used. By this time the leader should be familiar enough with the questioning to evolve a session with a picture of his own choice.

Method

I have included suggestions for one picture only. Depending on how successful the children are in relating to the picture, it might be possible to build a whole session around this one picture. Again, perhaps several would be needed.

Discussion with the children might pursue the following:

Does anyone have an idea about what the word *mood* means? (At this point, and similarly throughout the semester, new words to be introduced should be put on the board, divided into syllables, and pronounced by the group. This is part of the emphasis on vocabulary of which they might otherwise remain unaware. The teacher and the children need to concentrate in a variety of ways on building competency in using labels, i.e., words to express ideas. The children could keep a "word book", or they may incorporate some of these new words into their spelling lists.)

That's right—it's a way of feeling. (Reinforce any answers which are related to the question.) How many different ways have you felt? Do you always feel the same way? What things make you feel different?

Here is a picture of a boy about your age. Where could he be? Near his home? Near other people?

Why is he calling? Who could he be calling? Is it just a friendly call, or is it something else? How do you know? How does he feel?

How can you tell he is afraid? Of what? Somebody? Something? Show me. What is that somebody or something going to do to him? Can you show us when you were afraid?

Could it be he is afraid of something in his mind? Have you ever been afraid of something that *wasn't*? What were you afraid of? What did you do? What did you say? Where did you go for help? Where did you actually *find* help?

Could you be the little boy? Do we need any other people? Who? Who could he have been with before he came here? Who might be waiting for him? Where? Who comes along this road? Who could come when he calls?

This would, in addition to mood evocation, give the children some practice in simple projection. They would be encouraged to work backwards and forwards from this point in time and to add characters. Peripheral developments would be encouraged.

Anticipated Realization of Goals

Perhaps the most important contribution of this session is to allow children to dramatize their fears and other intense emotions without censure. Children need this chance to act out feelings which, for a variety of reasons, are often repressed. While another photograph might elicit more positive (happy) responses than the one used in this plan, this picture is entirely appropriate and should stimulate a good session.

By this midpoint in the series, children have been introduced *directly* to 1) rhythmic movement, both interpretive and abstract, 2) characterization, and 3) mood interpretation.

The children *may* also have developed spontaneously some feel for plot extension and dialogue. In the remaining five sessions the sequence pace is increased as the children are motivated to work with these competencies and to develop the ability to handle dialogue, to develop plot, and to integrate all of these into a unified improvisation.

Departure Point Six

Group Goals

1. To reinforce in children's minds that spontaneous drama works with many materials. This is a repetition of material (a fairy tale) and a repetition of subject (combination of people and animals).
2. To acquaint the children with another fairy tale and to introduce them to the writing of Hugh Lofting. Throughout the year the teacher and the children discuss writers in a very casual manner. Often, when children are particularly impressed with a book, they are also interested in the author; the teacher can encourage this interest, perhaps even encouraging children to write a letter of appreciation to an author.
3. To present a very funny, fanciful tale to the children, to counter-balance the previous session, which could have been quite sombre because of the picture chosen for motivation.

Drama Goals

1. To present to the children a choice of animal or person for interpretation.
2. To give the children further chance to build a character in relation to other characters.
3. To let the children begin some simple plot extension.

Materials

The material for this session is "The Story of Mrs. Tubbs," available in Arbuthnot's anthology on page 289.

Method

The teacher could begin discussion with the following:

Today we are going to work with a story which is somewhat like a fairy tale—only it doesn't happen long, long ago, as most fairy tales do. As you listen, see if you can tell *when* it happens.
    There are four people in the story: an old lady, Mrs. Tubbs; a dog, Peter Punk; a duck, Polly Ponk; and a pig, Patrick Pink. When we are finished with the story, perhaps some of you would like to be one of the people in the story.

The story is too long to be used as is for spontaneous dramatics motivation. Perhaps the teacher will share the story in a listening or other sharing period. He will want to condense it, perhaps using only part of the action or the *units of action* (see pages 124–125).
    The teacher, after sharing the story with the children, should first discuss what happened in it—a short review of the plot—then ask questions which could add depth of character and make the children more interested in the story:

Do we have ideas about what kind of woman Mrs. Tubbs was? What things make you think so? Did she have any family—sons or daughters who were grown up?
    How might she have gotten the animals? Why do you suppose they liked staying with her? Why were they so concerned about her when she was turned out of her house?
    How did they look as they walked away from their home? Can you show us? Do you think they looked differently when they walked back to the house the next morning? Who could show us that? How might the nephew have walked? Did he *swagger*? (Discuss meaning of word with children.) Can someone show us?

What might have happened if Mrs. Tubbs could not have gotten back into her house? Where are some places she could have lived? Would she have been comfortable? Could the animals have stayed there with her? Where might they have found food?

Which of the animals seems to be the cleverest? Why do you think so? Who could be one of the animals? (This leads into a dramatization of the story. Simple dramatization of the story might take one session; the plot extension, in the form of children's suggestions for other ways to eliminate the nephew, might take a second period.)

Perhaps simple movement activities might be a better way to lead into a dramatization for some groups; the leader could pursue such questions as:

Could you be the pig gathering *truffles* (a good vocabulary word to pursue)? The dog fishing? The duck making the bed?
Can you think of some other ways to get the nephew out of the house? How? What things would you need to accomplish this?

Depending on how long this procedure took and how involved the children became, the teacher would decide either to use or to hold until next session the questions designed to stimulate children to create further attempts to restore Mrs. Tubbs to her home.

As there is quite a difference in the sizes of the roles in the story, (e.g., between the pig and the swallow), probably the group will want to play this several times so each person has a chance at both kinds of roles.

Units of Action

For use in a spontaneous dramatics context, the story will need to be shortened considerably. It takes, uncut, approximately sixteen minutes to tell. As this is too long to spend in motivation, following is an analysis of the units of action in the story. Again, as it is a piece of literature by a significant author, the teacher would want to make sure to share the story in its entirety sometime with the children. Much of the detail in it, e.g., the duck saving her feathers under her "lavendar bonnet" and the dog using the pig as a hot water bottle for the old lady, are simply too delightful for the children to miss, even though they are not useable in this context. However, the teacher, using the following analysis, can practice telling the story in a shortened version, thereby making it possible to use it for spontaneous dramatics.

1. Mrs. Tubbs, a very old woman living on a small rented farm with a pig, a duck, and a dog, is evicted by the nephew of the owner, who comes to the farm to live.
2. The four friends pack up and set out late one evening. They walk through the falling leaves in the forest for a long time.
3. The animal friends are concerned because the lady is so old, and it is getting towards winter. They find a cave in which to spend the night, and then get some supper ready. They make a cozy bed of duck feathers in the cave for the old lady.
4. The next morning, before the old lady awakens, the three animals set off back in the direction of the farm, hoping an idea will occur to them.
5. They happen upon Tommy Squeak, King of the Water-Rats. They catch him and make him agree to help them. He has to do this because the old lady has helped him previously.
6. All the water rats attack the house, rattling pans, pulling the stuffing out of chairs, eating holes in the nephew's clothes. Unfortunately, the nephew orders a van of cats from London, so the rats are driven away.
7. Then the animal friends see Tilly Twitter, Queen of the Swallows, who also owes the old lady a favor. She and all her swallows harrass the nephew for several days. They stop up the chimney, put mud on the windows, and take straw from the barn and scatter it over the house; however, to no avail—the cats chase them away.
8. While the duck and pig return to the cave to care for the old lady, the dog stays behind to think. To help him think, the dog decides to retrieve an old bone, cached in a hollow tree.
9. Removing the bone disturbs a nest of wasps, who fly out to sting the dog. This is the solution! He runs into the house, leading the wasps into it, and they attack the nephew and drive him from the house. The little old lady is free to return to her home.

Anticipated Realization of Goals

The children will probably be interested enough by the story to enjoy dramatizing it (with emphasis on characterization) for at least one session. But further, the teacher will wish to develop in them an understanding that they can take a story and expand it by adding new incidents to it. This is a lead to the next session, in which they will have to create a whole situation, and to the last session, in which the adventures of Miss Price become the most important part of the dramatic experience. This is the beginning of creating a sustained dramatic incident, and as many sessions as deemed necessary could be spent on it.

Additional Sources

Other stories by Hugh Lofting which could be shared with the children, either with adaptations during dramatics sessions or uncut in a literature period, include:

Doctor Dolittle and the Green Canary. Philadelphia: Lippincott, 1950.
Doctor Dolittle and the Secret Lake. Philadelphia: Lippincott, 1948.
Doctor Dolittle in the Mood. Philadelphia: Lippincott, 1928.
Doctor Dolittle and the Caravan. Philadelphia: Lippincott, 1926.
Doctor Dolittle's Circus Philadelphia: Lippincott, 1924.
Doctor Dolittle's Garden. Philadelphia: Lippincott, 1927.
Doctor Dolittle's Post Office. Philadelphia: Lippincott, 1923.
Doctor Dolittle's Return. Philadelphia: Lippincott, 1933.
Doctor Dolittle's Zoo. Philadelphia: Lippincott, 1925.
The Story of Doctor Dolittle. Philadelphia: Lippincott, 1920.

Departure Point Seven

Group Goals

1. To give the children further experience in creating their own dramatic materials. (The picture included is quite specific. Because it deals with one person, the chance for *characterization* is great! It is, however, in some respects more limited than the materials in session eight, which will give the children a whole culture to work with.)
2. To encourage intelligent speculation about a person's character on the basis of limited clues, especially physical characteristics.

Drama Goals

1. To give children further experience in creating an improvisation about a person. This may or may not involve adding other people and dialogue and/or some simple extension of plot.
2. To lay the groundwork for session eight, in which the children will have a more complex and abstract stimulus from which to create a dramatization.

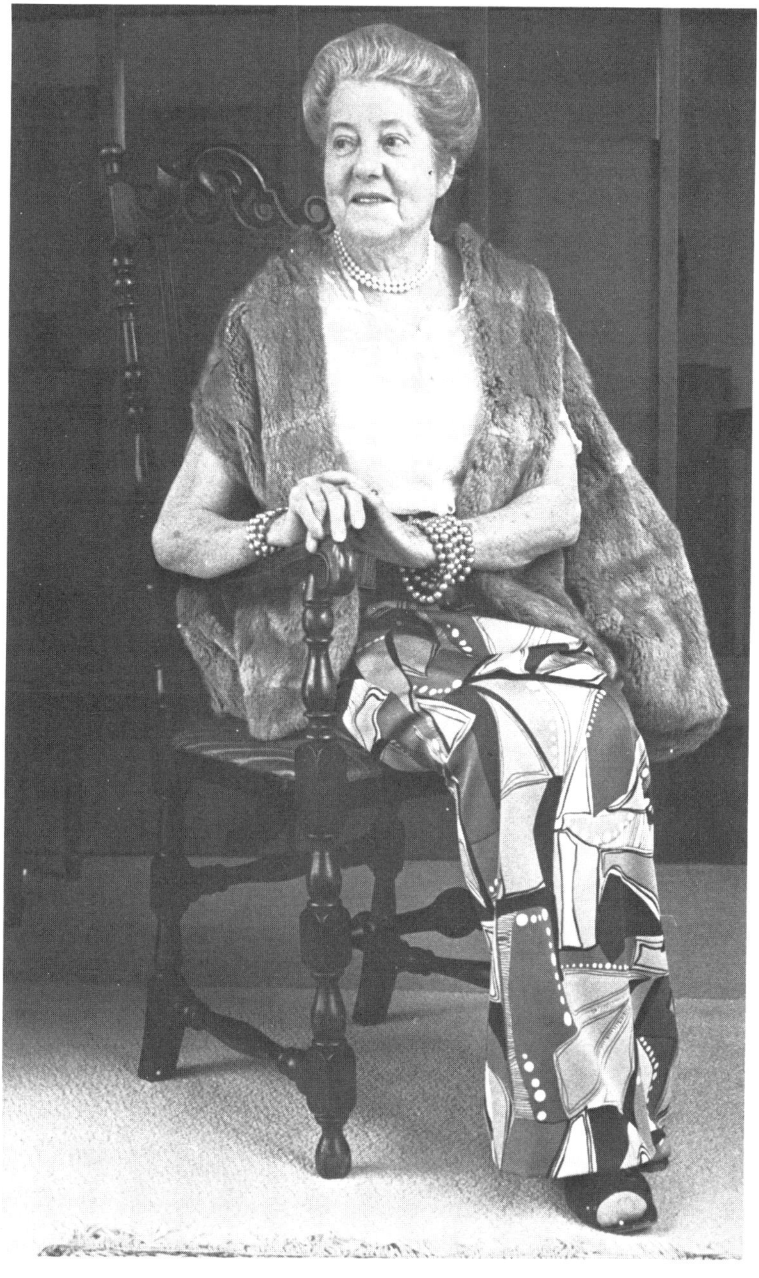

128   A Suggested Sequence of Spontaneous Dramatics

Materials

All questions in this section are keyed to the picture on page 127. Naturally, the leader is encouraged to search out other pictures and apply the questioning techniques to them.

Method

The leader could begin discussion with the following:

This time we're going to concentrate on just one person, rather than a whole set of people like we did last time. But, by the time we finish, we may need to talk about others.

Think about the lady in the picture. Who do you think she could be? Why is she all dressed up? Where could she be going? Is she going alone? How might she get there? If she is going with someone, what might the other person or persons look like?

What kind of occasion could it be? How can you tell? What things might they do when they get there? (This presents an opportunity for the children to dramatize some possibilities.) Do you like the lady? Why? What does she do? Work? At what? What did she do before she got ready? Did she see any people earlier in the day? Who? What did they do?

What kind of a home could she have? Does she live there with a family? What do they do? Is she nice to them? Is she usually nice to people? How can you tell? What things does she do that are nice?

After this, or a similar discussion, children should be ready to start interpreting various aspects of her life and the lives of those around her. The teacher and children could work backwards and forwards in time from the moment of the picture.

While these will begin as fragmentary, discontinuous improvisations on various aspects of her life, perhaps eventually they could be pulled together into a continuous sequence of events, to make a story with a beginning, a middle, and an end.

The other people in her life would probably involve the boys in the group. It may be difficult to get the boys to empathize with this particular picture. There is the possibility that in using this material it would be wiser to divide the group into two halves, boys and girls, instead of having one heterogeneous group. A different material could be used with the group of boys. Such decision would have to be made after knowing an actual group and their characteristics.

Anticipated Realization of Goals

Having had several opportunities to work out characterization and to develop or extend story lines, the children now should be fairly competent in expressing their ideas and in choosing effective means for communicating them.

Departure Point Eight

Group Goals

1. To correlate materials presented in dramatics with other areas of study. Children in elementary school, in their social studies classes, frequently study the culture of one or more groups of people throughout the world. Such study will provide a good lead into this session. In addition, they can devote much time in the language arts class to writing stories about the topic.
2. To increase skills of cooperation.

Drama Goals

1. To present to the children pictures which will stimulate them to create a dramatization of life in an unnamed culture. The picture will be the only stimulus. The children will have to develop all the rest for themselves.
2. To *continue* developing in children increasing competency in manipulating the dramatic elements to create and play a story of their own devising.

Materials

This session will be concerned with the picture on page 130. Other useful pictures could be found in either Kari Hunt and Bernice W. Carlson, *Masks and Mask Makers* (Nashville: Abingdon Press, 1961) or Matthew Baranski, *Mask Making* (Worcester: Davis Press, 1962).

The basic idea is to use a picture stimulus of another culture to motivate children. Any material can accomplish this purpose, so the teacher is encouraged to select something else if he wishes. Old copies of *National Geographic* may also serve as a good source.

Another possibility to explore would be using a film to motivate dramatics with children. The teacher might try using the *Loon's Necklace* (Encyclopedia Britannica, 10m, sound and color). It is a sensitive recreation of an old Indian legend involving a medicine man and a loon.

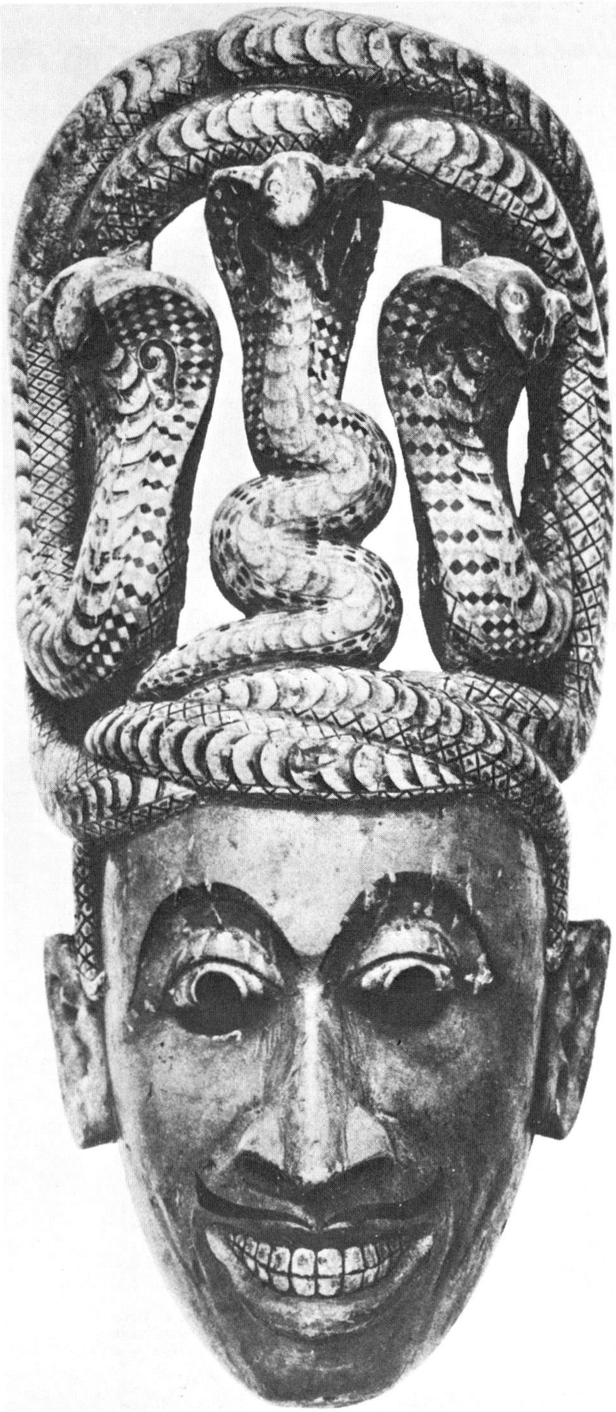

Method

A discussion with the children could deal with some or many of the following questions and would be a stimulus to the children to create small, impromptu playing of ideas, which would lead gradually into the creation of a full-scale improvisation dealing with some aspect of the lives of the creators of these artifacts:

This mask is from a people living a long way from here. Can you look at it and tell me anything about the people who made the mask?

What is the mask made of? How is it painted? Is it realistic? For what purposes could it be used?

We don't know much about the people who made the mask. Can you imagine where they might live? How? Villages? Family units like ours? Many or few children?

What could their homes be like? What are they made of? Does everyone make his own, or does everybody help each other? Where are the homes located in relation to the rest of the village?

What kind of cooking facilities could they have? What kinds of food might they eat? How is it prepared? (At any point in the procedure the children can begin improvising, e.g., girls might do a scene about the kitchen.) How do the men provide the food? How might this affect their way of life?

Are there schools for the children? Who teaches them? What kinds of materials do they use? How long do the children go to school? Could you show us what kinds of activities go on in the school?

What are the villages like? Do people exchange goods or services, or are they quite independent? Are there roads? How do people get around? Do they go from village to village? Could this be dangerous? For what reasons? (This might make an especially good departure point!)

What do people look like? How do they dress? Why? What are their clothes made of? How do they wear their hair? (All of this is related to the concept usually developed in children's social studies class that people often tell their occupations by what they wear.)

At any point in this discussion the children would be encouraged to begin dramatizing their answers. Gradually, these can string together and finally work into a coherent improvisation about some aspect of life in this unidentified community. While the teacher should not push this particular aspect, the improvisations might revolve around the happenings of a child, due to the age of the improvisers. The children might

132 A Suggested Sequence of Spontaneous Dramatics

be interested in developing this child into quite a distinct personality, another good exercise in characterization. This personification could lead to an interesting series of adventures for the child.

Anticipated Realization of Goals

By this time in the sequence, the children should be quite confident in their own abilities to do dramatics. As children are often anxious to share things they have learned, this time they could be allowed to share the improvisation with another class, if it seems feasible. The teacher will be able to tell if the group is at a point at which sharing their improvisations with an audience would not interfere with the children's spontaneity and innovativeness.

It should be noted that the motivational materials are from actual native cultures; however, these will not be identified for the children at this point. They are groups with which the children probably will not be familiar, but this was planned purposefully. Having had no contact with these cultures, the children will feel completely free to create any kind of story they wish. At another time, the "correct" information about these people can be shared with the children.

Departure Point Nine

Group Goals

1. To encourage cooperation among the children in the group composition of a dramatic sequence motivated by a picture.
2. To impress upon the children again that, often in the art of spontaneous dramatics, the participants create the material.

Drama Goals

1. To give children a chance to act out the material they have created. This will involve manipulating characterization, plot, dialogue, and mood.

Materials

All questions in this session are concerned with the picture on page 133. Again, the leader is free to substitute.

Method

The leader could introduce the picture with something similar to the following:

Last time we worked with creating a dramatic incident about a mask. This time we have even less to start us thinking. Look at this picture. Just some chairs. It doesn't tell us much, or does it?

Where could this be? How do you know? What kind of a forest is it? Is it far away from the cities? How does one get there? Does anyone, or anything live in the forest? Who? Are they friendly? To everybody? (There would be a chance here for children to begin some simple improvisations.)

For what reasons might the chairs be in the forest? Who could have put them there? What kinds of people might be coming? Why did they decide to meet in the forest? For what purposes are they coming together? Are there only four, or are more people coming? Men or women? How old? Do they meet often? In other places? Have they been coming here long? Why did they choose this particular type of chair?

Is there anybody who would rather they didn't meet? Why? Is their reason for coming here a good one? Will everyone be happy about what they decide?

Could we use some of these ideas to create a story we could act out?

As the discussion proceeds, the teacher will encourage the children to improvise the responses. By the end of the session, he will have been able to help the children to put together many seemingly unrelated ideas into a coherent story line. By this stage in their experience with dramatics, the children should be ready to create a sustained dramatic incident, in all ways like a play, except for the lack of a written script.

Anticipated Realization of Goals

Goals for this session are the same as they were for session eight.

Departure Point Ten

Group Goals

1. To develop in children increased confidence in their ability to express ideas, develop story line, and relate their interpretations to the work of others.
2. To increase ability to work together in planning the extension of a story line and to create new characters to change plot.

Drama Goals

1. To provide the children with an interesting modern fairy tale, the playing of which will allow them to use the many abilities they have developed in previous sessions.

Materials

The story, which is analyzed on the following pages, is Mary Norton, *The Magic Bed-Knob* (New York: Hyperion Press, 1943). It is also available in abbreviated form in Arbuthnot's anthology, p. 326.

The story is analyzed very completely in order to show the many elements that may be used in working with the children. The leader may not choose to analyze other stories as completely as this or to use all of the ideas presented here, but this provides a sample of the type of material found in good stories.

Method

1. The leader first should read the story completely through, using a variety of voices, but not stopping to discuss it.

2. Discussion of the people in the story: How did they look? Feel? Move? Did this change at various times? Could you be Miss Price? On her broomstick? Could you be Paul?
3. Providing this went well, the teacher would then lead a discussion of the action of the story. What happened? When? Why? What might of happened if ...?
4. Putting the people and the action together, the children would then dramatize the story; this would undoubtedly take a complete period, perhaps longer.
5. After brief remotivation, the following period the teacher could give the children a chance to begin on the adventures of the traveling bed, which might well take several periods.
6. When the teacher has decided that the group has used this story as much as possible, he would read the rest of the story to the children, as part of their experiences in literature during story time.

Characters

1. *Miss Price* is a fastidious maiden lady who is diligently practicing to be a witch.
2. *Agnes* is a village girl who serves as Miss Price's maid for a few hours a day.
3. *Paul* is a light sleeper who has discovered Miss Price practicing broomstick-riding in the moonlight.
4. *Carey,* and
5. *Charles,* brother and sister of Paul, have discovered Paul's secret knowledge about Miss Price.
6. *Aunt Beatrice* is a well-intentioned (and gullible) present-sender, who thinks Miss Price really *did* sprain her ankle in a fall from a bicycle.

Units of Action

Before the story action actually begins, three things have taken place:

1. Paul has seen Miss Price practicing to be a witch. (This episode is related incidentally, after the main action is underway.) He had been awakened several times at night by the moonlight, and one particular night he saw his neighbor riding a broom.
2. Miss Price, during one of her practice sessions, lost her balance and fell from the broomstick. Paul also saw this lack of skill, which resulted in the broken ankle.

3. Paul has told the other children, Carey and Charles, his secret, and their curiosity has been aroused.

The story actually begins as Carey finally thinks up a somewhat reasonable excuse to go see Miss Price. It would be thoughtful, Carey reasons, to take Miss Price a basketful of peaches.

Later that afternoon the children are ushered into Miss Price's sitting room and accept her offer to stay to tea. After some polite small talk, Carey compulsively confronts her with their awareness of her activities.

Without thinking carefully, Miss Price agrees to do a bit of magic to show the children that she is, indeed, on her way to becoming a witch. She changes Paul into a little yellow frog, then back again. Then, to her horror, she realizes her secret is out. How can she silence the children?

The realization that she may not be able to continue her studies in privacy causes Miss Price to become quite unpleasant; she ponders an evil spell for the children. Carey comes up with a pleasant alternative, which results in a whole new set of adventures for the children and maintained secrecy for Miss Price.

Dramatic Elements

1. *Plot.* The plot has been summarized in the units of action above. I have purposely left out some elements in order to arouse your curiosity in the story.

2. *Characterizations.* The central character, Miss Price, is drawn very completely, and children find her interesting as she bears some similarities to Mary Poppins. Miss Price is shown as:

   a. *conscientious*—Paul has seen her practicing many times.
   b. *well-respected*—the people in the community, e.g., Aunt Beatrice, are concerned that she has sprained her ankle.
   c. *fastidious*—references are made to her "neat front door," "tidy hair," and "spotlessly clean" house.
   d. *financially comfortable*—she is able to retain a maid, Agnes.
   e. *sympathetic to children*—she teaches them a game and lends Paul a book.
   f. *modest*—when asked if she is a witch, she hesitates to say she is, as she is still learning.
   g. *competent*—she has progressed far enough to turn Paul into a frog, which certainly indicates some basic ability in witching.

A Suggested Sequence of Spontaneous Dramatics 137

  h. *talented*—she has taken piano lessons and even sings at church concerts.
  i. *realistic*—she knows her limitations. The slave the children request she recognizes as clearly beyond her abilities, at least at the moment.
  j. *reasonable*—she is willing to make use of the children's suggestions when unable to come up with a better one of her own.

Miss Price's motivation during the story is unwavering; it is directed entirely at becoming a very good witch. After an early life restricted by piano lessons and "looking after my mother," she is trying very hard to make up for lost time. Becoming a witch must be a lengthy process, because at one point she remarks, "I started too late in life." Being wicked evidently will remain beyond her always.

Her secondary motivation is to silence the children, who, by telling what they have seen, will spoil her chances to pursue her hobby in privacy. This knowledge makes her desperate and, for a while, this is her primary motivation, but Carey's rational suggestion allows her to continue work on her project.

Paul, who shares second billing with his sister Carey, is characterized as a thoughtful child. Further, he is:

  a. *trustworthy*—it is only after some coercion of unspecified nature that he relinquishes his secret about Miss Price.
  b. *unselfish*—he takes much pride in Miss Price's increasing proficiency in flying. Once, when she did a particularly good maneuver, "Paul nearly clapped."
  c. *introspective*—while other children play backgammon, he is more interested in an illustrated volume of *Paradise Lost*.
  d. *encouraging*—when the others question Miss Price's ability to make magic while recovering, Paul asserts that "She could do it lying down . . ."
  e. *typically-drawn*—as the little boy with his pockets full of miscellany, he is the one who provides the bed-knob.

Paul's motivation changes upon the discovery that the other children know of Miss Price's secret. Until this time his objective, which he has been accomplishing quite successfully, was to observe and enjoy vicariously Miss Price's project of mastering witchery.

After Carey and Charles have discovered what he knows, Paul's motivation becomes that of proving to them that Miss Price is indeed a witch. There are earlier indications (e.g., ". . . that they would have said at once, 'Don't be silly, Paul' ") that the children do not believe all that he says. His question to Miss Price when they are in her sitting room reflects his desire to prove that he has not been making up stories. Of the older children, Carey is more carefully delineated than Charles. It is she who makes the positive suggestion accepted by Miss Price which saves them from a wicked spell. Though she serves this very useful purpose, she remains secondary to Paul and Miss Price.

Carey and Charles are sketched very lightly, the main distinguishing characteristic they share is the typical browbeating of a younger child. This is indicated at various spots in the story:

"... tackled Paul."
"... you ought to have told us ... It was mean of you, Paul."
"... it was really very selfish ..."
"... but was silenced by a kick from Charles ..."
"Oh, don't be silly Paul."

The brother and sister's motivation is very simplistic—to find out if Miss Price's preoccupation is with witchcraft, and to have some demonstration of her ability. They pursue this until they convince her to show them. When Miss Price realizes she has betrayed herself, she turns disagreeable. Carey's motivation then changes to a desire to protect them from her. Charles, through inaction, ceases at this point to be significant to the story line.

Probably the fact that there is not much detail in the characterization is good, as it leaves room for the children in the class to individualize them.

Similarly, the characters of Agnes and Aunt Beatrice are mere outlines. They serve their functional purposes and depart from the scene. There are many ways in which these two could be developed and, indeed, made to serve pivotal purposes. (Some of these ways are suggested in the section *Character Multiplication* on page 141. Children working with the story could come up with many more ways.)

3. *Dialogue.* The dialogue occurs essentially in three parts:

a. the opening section involving the children, in which Carey and Charles reprimand Paul for not sharing his information.
b. a short, linking section in which Carey and Charles think up the logical excuse to go to visit Miss Price.
c. the conversation which ensues when the children arrive at Miss Price's home.

In the first section, the dialogue is primarily of value in establishing Paul's relationships with the other children. The other action is recounted primarily in narrative.

The middle section dialogue is primarily functional and does not include any particularly descriptive passages; therefore, it is not helpful in establishing either character or mood.

The third section fills out our picture of Miss Price begun by the narrative in section one. Through the dialogue we discover that Miss Price is gracious, conscious of family obligations, nervous when frightened, mean when threatened, and, finally (in her warning to the children as they leave), a moderate person. All of this is learned through dialogue, rather than through narrative.

4. *Theme.* The theme is a dramatization of conflict between man and a force larger than himself, namely society. While there is some immediate element of conflict between man and man (in the threat which the children pose to Miss Price), they are really only symbolic of the danger Miss Price faces if society (her neighbors) should discover her endeavor.

5. *Rhythm.* The story begins briskly, with the children intently questioning Paul about what he has seen. There is a brief interlude of relaxation, in which Paul's nightly watching is related in narrative. The scene at the lunch table picks up the pace again and, from then on, there is little relaxation until the climax of the story. Though the children have tea, which provides another slight release of the tension, underlying the whole scene is the awareness that sooner or later one of them will be driven to asking Miss Price "The Question." After Miss Price's revelation, the tempo increases furiously, until the climax is reached in her acceptance of the suggestion. The tension relaxes in a fairly long coda, and the children start home.

6. *Mood (or Atmosphere).* The author sets the story by establishing an eerie mood in which Paul watches Miss Price practice. He watches "... with his eyes fixed on the pale sky beyond the ragged blackness of the cedar boughs."

The middle section, as in other respects, is passed over lightly, being simply a convenience to carry the reader along. The only descriptive material is the "... high, dark dining room."

A very complete picture is presented when we come to the section dealing with tea at Miss Price's. We have many descriptive passages:

"neat front door"
"path ... gaily bordered with flowers"
"dimity curtains"
"little sitting room"

"little table . . . for the tea-tray, a white cloth on the table for scones, bread and margarine, the quince jelly and the utility cake"

A mood of happiness and unsuspecting pleasantness is established, which is an effective contrast to the later suspense. The suspense is well established, e.g., "A bumblebee came in through the window and buzzed heavily in the room. Except for this the silence was complete."

Needs in the Story

1. We will consider *physical needs* on the assumption that there will be some minimal use of location and props to aid the improvising of the story. If materials are to be used, the story requires some simple props, e.g., a broom, a basket of fruit, tables, and chairs. Since the location of each of the three major scenes is never revisited, the same working space could be used, by just making some simple furniture substitutions.

2. *Dramatic-emotional needs* are apparent in the story and, perhaps, it would be good to talk with the children about where the emotional climax of the story is located. The teacher asks such questions as:

What is the most important thing that happens?
When does it happen? Where? Who is there?
Do you know what intense means?
Have you ever felt intense? Why do the children feel this way?
How could we make the moment more scary than it is?
Through our actions? Our bodies? Our faces? Through what we make up to say?
How can we show we are relaxed afterwards? Can you feel relaxed inside yourself? Would that help you to look relaxed outside?

Another dramatic need of the story is to establish the character of Miss Price as benign. This is done through the children's and Aunt Beatrice's descriptions of her. It is also established in order to emphasize the horror of the children when she does come up with a wicked idea. Contrasting this with her earlier character can be most effective.

3. The *social needs* of the play change considerably when the idea of an evil spell occurs to Miss Price. Until this time, the children have had no need to act as a group. At her suggestion they coalesce; they need to work together to avoid the dire consequences. Indeed, Paul proves himself a valued member of the group by producing the bed-knob which is to save them from the spell. Here again, the leader could talk with the children to help to establish this feeling:

How did the children feel when Miss Price thought of the evil spell?
How could the children protect themselves? What might they do with their bodies? What could they say?
How did the others feel about Carey when she made the suggestion? How could they show how they felt?
How did the children react when Paul produced the bed-knob? Were they pleased? Did they let him know?

Another social need is that of Miss Price wanting to maintain her present role in the community. Again, some questions may help:

What do people think of Miss Price?
Have they felt this way for a long time?
Why do they feel this way? Why does she want them to continue?
How do people usually react to witches?
What might their reaction be if they found out about Miss Price? What would they say? What might they do?

Character Multiplication

The characters in the story could be multiplied in at least two ways:

1. Through *expansion,* by adding substance to the minor characters to make them more interesting. Both Aunt Beatrice and Agnes are "place holders," i.e., they serve a useful purpose but do not assume an importance as people. It would be possible to build both of them into real characters and, perhaps, some inventive child could actually make them become significant to changing the flow of the plot.

2. Through *addition,* by adding characters somehow related to the present characters. For example, there could easily be one more child. Aunt Beatrice could have a husband, or the children could be living with their parents. There could be a family pet. Perhaps some other children could discover the secret. Miss Price could be living with a maiden sister. More significantly, the person with whom she is studying to be a witch could be introduced. She undoubtedly needs a teacher for the more involved aspects of witching, and this would make a wonderful part for some child to create. During the children's visit, some townspeople could also drop in to visit which could provide some additional "improvisation" possibilities.

Scene Expansion

This is perhaps the most significant reason for choosing the story as it appears—it could be just the beginning of a whole series of improvisations. As the story closes, the children are going happily homeward, with the brass bed-knob clutched tightly in Paul's hand; they are ready to try their luck at the traveling bed. Nothing is said of their further adventures; any group of children could come up with a myriad of ideas about what would happen and where they would go. The story, for telling purposes, comes to a conclusion at this point. By condensing this in a short remotivation during the second session, the leader could stimulate interest in going on a new adventure with the bed.

In addition, the discovery by Charles and Carey of Miss Price's endeavor, related only briefly in the story, could be dramatized fully, perhaps even including a scene in which Paul would show them Miss Price in her practice session. The dining room scene at home is equally brief and could be expanded to allow more three-dimensional parts for the aunt and for the uncle she might acquire in the improvisation.

Anticipated Realization of Goals

By the time the material in this session has been reached, the children should have developed a flexible capability in spontaneous dramatics which will allow them to work with any materials for stimulus. There are numerous suggestions in the foregoing description about where the ideas in this session might lead.

Additional Sources

Other stories by Mary Norton to be used with the children, either as spurs to spontaneous dramatics or in the literature sharing periods, include:

Bed-Knob and Broomstick. New York: Harcourt Brace Jovanovich, 1957.
Borrowers. New York: Harcourt Brace Jovanovich, 1953.
The Borrowers Afield. New York: Harcourt Brace Jovanovich, 1955.
The Borrowers Afloat. New York: Harcourt Brace Jovanovich, 1959.
The Borrowers Aloft. New York: Harcourt Brace Jovanovich, 1961.

6

Reference Lists

This chapter is, in the best sense of the word, a potpourri—a collection of materials which may be of use to the drama leader. Because it is my belief that one can never know about *too many* resources, the chapter is extensive and, unlike the other chapters, it should probably not be read through in its entirety. Rather, it is designed as a resource to which you can go for new ideas, sources, and encouragement.

Because lists usually make dull reading, and also because titles are frequently either uninspired or inadequate descriptions of content, all of the references have been annotated. These annotations are brief, but it is hoped they will whet your appetite, so you will want to do further reading in the many helpful materials which are included and/or to make use of the resources in your classroom.

The following types of materials are included:

1. Books of interest to the adult reader.
2. Pamphlets and other occasional materials about drama for the adult leader.
3. A list of periodical articles about creative dramatics in many subject matter areas.
4. Books from the field of children's literature which are useful as motivation for spontaneous drama.
5. Records which provide aural stimulation for children.
6. Films about drama.
7. Poems which are particularly good for use in spontaneous dramatics.
8. Suggestions for visual motivations for children in drama.

None of the materials included earlier in the book are listed here. Those materials were annotated when first mentioned, and no attempt has been made to compile a comprehensive list.

List One

The books in this list can extend your knowledge of dramatics with children. In a real sense, no *one* book can adequately deal with all the facets of any topic, so it is my suggestion that after reading one book you sample other authors' ideas about dramatics. You'll discover that in this, as in other subject areas, there are areas of agreement, but also areas of disagreement, which is healthy, as stimuli to thought. Reading some of the books on this list should cause you to reexamine what you believe, rethink what I have said here, and reevaluate what you do with children.

1. Burger, Isabel. *Creative Play Acting—Learning Through Drama,* 2nd ed. Baltimore: Children's Theatre Association, 1963. This book sets forth practical procedures for organizing and developing a creative dramatics project. Beginning with an appraisal of the contributions of play acting to the emotional development of the child, the book shows step-by-step progress from simple pantomine to complete play, with suggested exercises classified according to age group and immediate objectives. It includes practical pointers on makeup, costuming, staging, and selection of materials.

2. Byers, Ruth. *Creating Theater.* San Antonio: Trinity University Press, 1968. Mrs. Byers states at the beginning of the book that her major interest is in experiences which "lead to play creation, writing and production." As such, the book is an extension of, rather than an explanation of, spontaneous dramatics. Her book is worthwhile reading, however, as it describes informal drama activities, and then moves to having the child write versions of his playing into a more permanent form. A unique aspect of the book is the inclusion of nine original plays written and produced at the Dallas Theater Center, where the author works.

3. Chambers, Dewey W. *Literature for Children: Storytelling and Creative Drama.* Pose Lamb, consulting ed. Dubuque, Iowa: William C. Brown, 1970. Chambers' book deals very satisfactorily with both arts included in the title and is, hence, of interest to an elementary school teacher. In the section devoted specifically to drama, the author identifies readiness activities leading into drama, describes procedures in planning the crucial first session, and relates at length the description of an actual fourth-grade work with an old folk tale. The drama leader will find both the section on classroom climate and on the steps involved in creative drama to be of help.

4. Cullum, Albert. *Push Back the Desks.* New York: Citation Press, 1967. While this book is only occasionally concerned with leading drama sessions, it

is a dynamic and captivating example of what a creative teacher can accomplish with children. Cullum, who writes in a very readable fashion, is a master at inventing compelling new approaches to teaching dull, old subject matter. It is strongly recommended for its spirit and élan, rather than for its specific drama techniques.

5. Hunt, Douglas and Kari Hunt. *Pantomine.* New York: Atheneum, 1964. In simple, nontechnical writing, which holds the interest even of one unfamiliar with mime, the authors explore the art from its earliest beginnings among prehistoric cave dwellers to its most recent manifestations on television. Though the chapters are brief (five to seven pages) and specific sources are not footnoted, each of the distinctive forms are treated in a believable and interesting way. The photographs included augment the text satisfactorily. I only wish the Hunts would have expanded the tantalizingly brief section entitled, "Try it Yourself." The book is possible for children with well-developed reading skills, and yet fascinating enough for even adults.

6. Kerman, Gertrude Lerner. *Plays and Creative Ways with Children.* Irvington-on-Hudson: Harvey House Publishers, 1961. Although this is an older book, it is one which can be of much help to a teacher who finds himself in the position of having to "put on" a play. Mrs. Kerman's title emphasizes the book's orientation—that of moving children through dramatics to drama; nonetheless, the sections on dramatics are helpful. I found the chapters on mood, dialogue, and characterization to be especially useful, and if one must put on a play, this collection of plays for children is probably as useful as any.

7. Marshall, Sybil. *An Experiment in Education.* Cambridge: The University Press, 1966. Mrs. Marshall's book, a spiritual descendent of earlier books by Natalie Cole, recounts the author's work in a small rural community school in Britain. Her integrated approach to learning was marked by a flexibility and ingeniousness which drama leaders could well emulate.

8. Siks, Geraldine Brain. *Children's Literature for Dramatization: An Anthology.* New York: Harper & Row, 1964. A collection of stories used during the author's twenty-year career of working in dramatics with children, the ones included in this book are among the most popular with children. The author has tightened the plots, eliminated unrelated descriptive material, and exerpted the most dramatic incidents from longer stories. The preface by Mrs. Siks, the introduction by a college drama department chairman, and the brief introductory notes for each selection make this far richer reading than just a simple anthology. A bibliography directs the reader to related material. The only drawback to the book is the lack of an index.

9. Siks, Geraldine Brain and Hazel Brain Dunnington, eds. *Children's Theatre and Creative Dramatics.* Seattle: University of Washington Press, 1961. The American Educational Theatre Association commissioned this contributed book to survey the state of the art and enlisted the aid of most of the leaders in the field, in order to examine the two parts of children's drama: children's theatre, and creative dramatics. Graham's chapter on the values of drama is a good basic statement, as is its companion piece by Eleanor York on the values of creative dramatics. Authors have examined creative dramatics in its various settings:

schools, churches, correctional institutions, and community and recreation programs. The main body of the book closes with a chapter on recommended training for a creative dramatics leader. The three appendixes will also prove helpful.

10. Tiedt, Iris M. and Sidney W. Tiedt. *Readings on Contemporary English in the Elementary School.* Englewood Cliffs, N.J.: Prentice-Hall, 1967. I would especially recommend "Learning Through Creative Dramatics" (pp. 36–44) by Margaret S. Woods. This is a good introductory article to those unfamiliar with the major ideas of dramatics and the writings of leaders in the area. Woods writes convincingly, especially of the conditions necessary to create a climate for the art. Beyond this article, however, this collection includes several articles of interest. Those by Evertts (on composition), Evans (on grammar), and Sawyer (story-telling) are but a few of the well-written materials helpfully compiled from a diversity of sources.

11. Ward, Winifred. *Playmaking with Children.* New York: Appleton-Century-Crofts, 1957. Although an older book now, this remains a basic reference source concerned with the entire scope of drama in schools. Ward's comments on the use of Shakespeare with young children are helpful. Appendix number two is an extremely useful list of stories with brief annotations arranged according to age levels. While many of the books referred to are undoubtedly now out of print, they would still be available in libraries, and teachers will find this list an invaluable source of ideas.

List Two

Frequently, very helpful ideas appear in neither books or periodical articles, but in what we have, for lack of a better term, called "occasional materials." Published at irregular intervals, these are sometimes difficult to locate, but are nevertheless worth the effort, as they can further your understanding of dramatics.

1. Harris, Peter, "Drama in Education," *English in Education* 1, No. 3 (Autumn 1967). A valuable article on drama in primary schools opens this comprehensive, yet small, publication which gives American readers an insight into the drama program in Great Britain. Teachers would find one article, "Sit Down, Sidney," to be particularly helpful, as it deals with children doing seated pantomimes—one solution to the problem of inadequate space. The article on improvisation by Dorothy Heathcote, a noted leader in the drama movement, is also of much interest. This publication is put out by the National Association for the Teaching of English, which is the British equivalent of our National Council of Teachers of English.

2. Hoetker, James. *Dramatics and the Teaching of Literature.* Champaign: National Council of Teachers of English, 1969. The author begins by pointing out how infrequently drama is an integral part of the American English class and follows this with a helpful chapter on drama as a part of British schools.

Another chapter describes, with extensive footnotes directing the reader to other sources, the various forms of drama: spontaneous and planned psychodrama, theatre games, creative dramatics, oral interpretation, readers' theatre, and play rehearsal. Hoetker concludes by pointing out the specific values from drama for students of varying intellectual levels in the schools.

3. Siks, Geraldine Brain. "Creative Dramatics for Children," publication in the series, *Contributions in Reading,* no. 26. Rev. ed. Lexington, Mass: Ginn and Company, 1965. A brief pamphlet from a helpful series by Ginn, this provides a concise introduction to the art. Mrs. Siks deals with a definition of the term, a rationale for the art as part of an elementary curriculum, and the means of guiding this creative process at both the primary and intermediate levels. You can send for a free copy of this and other leaflets in the series which deal with many aspects of the language arts program.

4. *English Encountered* (March 1964, December 1964, February 1967, May 1967, February 1968), Wisconsin English-Language Arts Project. A series of monthly newsletters, edited by several different people and dealing with all aspects of the language arts, this source is practically oriented with many ideas for the classroom teacher. Some of the materials were incorporated into the Wisconsin English Curriculum Project (Director, Robert C. Pooley), also available from the Wisconsin Department of Public Instruction in Madison.

List Three

The advantages of periodical articles are twofold:

1. They present readers with the most recent ideas and materials which have not yet been included in books.
2. They present detailed considerations of some aspects of a more general topic which have not been examined elsewhere.

The articles in this list, which is rather selective, have been chosen because they augment and extend some of the ideas we have been considering, or because they deal in a fresh way with ideas not considered in this book.

1. Allen, Joan Gore. "Creative Dramatics and Language Arts Skills," *Elementary English* 46 (April 1969): 436–437. The writer reports on her work with a fourth-grade class which wrote a play from a story, of the learnings generated in this activity, and of her belief that teachers do not need to lay down formal rules for this procedure. She feels students, when involved, do not realize the amount of work they are doing as part of the enjoyable activities.

2. Allyon, Maurie and Susan Snyder. "Behavioral Objectives in Creative Dramatics," *Journal of Educational Research* 62, no. 8 (April 1969): 355–359. The authors measured children's overt response to two different types of stimuli; verbal clues and a student model. They found that the more verbal clues given,

the more overt behaviors children exhibit; no attempt was made to determine the quality of the behaviors. In the second experiment, children watched a child model (high or low responder on the previous experiment) and then responded themselves. When a high-response model was used, the children made more responses than when a low-response model was used. Again, no assessment of quality was made. The research is limited by the small number of subjects and the artificiality of the situation; children worked alone, not in groups.

3. Brady, Bee. "The Play's Not the Thing," *Grade Teacher* 85 (March 1968): 82–83. Brady begins her article by identifying several purposes for creative drama. She advocates using stories to motivate; she feels pictures are too static. However, her recommendations for how to choose a story are valuable. Kipling and Stevenson stories are recommended.

4. Burger, Isabel. "Creative Dramatics: An Educational Tool," *Instructor* 73 (September 1963); 133–136. Burger's definition of improvisation begins the article: "[It is] the expression of thought and feeling in one's own terms, through action, the spoken word, or both." She recommends beginning with the total group in pantomine, and she offers to children two helpful keys to success: 1) make a picture in your mind, and 2) think the thoughts of the character you are being.

5. Caffier, Blanche Hutchings. "Science Teaching Through Creative Dramatics," *Grade Teacher* 78 (April 1961): 50. Mrs. Caffier reports her work on the cycle from frog's eggs to tadpoles to frogs, done with her first-grade group. The idea for the project came from children after one child found some eggs in a pond, and she describes the group's planning of their ideas on a chart before the playing. She recommends using "Toads" (Dowling Pictures) as a supplementary aid.

6. Calabria, Frances. "The Why of Creative Dramatics," *Instructor* 77 (August 1967): 182. In this article Calabria begins by defining creativity as taking "... known bits of information, and putting them together in a way no one has thought of before." She then goes on to show how drama lends itself to this process. She speaks convincingly of the reasons for doing dramatics, including the help it offers in perfecting speaking and listening skills.

7. Catalano, Joseph. "Why Not Teach Them Drama?" *Instructor* 80 (April 1971): 92–93. The author, concerned primarily with planning drama experiences for very young children, describes his approach and the rules which govern it. The importance of eurythmics is emphasized. The article is full of concrete suggestions aimed at using drama with five year olds.

8. Davis, Sandra S. "Pied Piper Way to Reading," *High Points* 50 (Winter 1968): 8–10. Working with comparable groups of intermediate grade children, this teacher provided drama and music activities leading to reading for one group; the other experienced a highly motivating program which did *not* include drama. Scores on a standardized reading test, administered at the close of a four-month treatment period, indicated that the group whose reading activities grew out of drama and music experiences scored higher than did the control group. The author had even achieved a statistically significant improvement in reading scores.

9. Dixon, John. "Creative Expression in Great Britain," *English Journal* 57 (September 1968): 795–802. Dixon discusses both creative writing and improvisation. He feels that the writing should use feelings, as well as thoughts, which arise from personal experiences. Improvisation helps students penetrate roles and, therefore, offers the possibility of changing their attitudes about subjects.

10. DuBois, Eloise Barclay. "Values and Techniques of Creative Dramatics," *Childhood Education* 47 (April 1971): 369–371. The author begins her article with suggestions for very simple drama techniques, including small group dialogues. She stresses the need for beginning work with small groups and increasing the group size as members become comfortable with drama. She warns against overdependency on seasonal motivations, because of children's stereotypic ideas about seasons and holidays.

11. Etter, Mary S. "Puppetry—A Means of Creativity in the Language Arts," *Virginia Journal of Education* 61 (November 1967): 13. Mrs. Etter reports of her work with *Many Moons* and the *Wizard of Oz* with fourth graders. She relates how they chose incidents in the stories, then wrote dialogue to dramatize them. Her report of work with marionettes is unique.

12. Fariday, M. J. "Creative Dramatics: An Exciting Newcomer in the Elementary Curriculum," *Minnesota Journal of Education* 48 (January 1968): 20–21. Mrs. Fariday reports the results of her work, primarily based on literature as a motivation. Her comments on evaluation after the session are helpful. She did an informal test of listening skills which revealed that listening improved after creative drama sessions and that the greatest amount of improvement occurred among academically slow children.

13. Fertik, M. I. "Crescendo: Creative Dramatics in Philadelphia," *Wilson Library Bulletin* 43 (October 1968): 160–164. The purpose of this project is to develop in children an awareness of themselves as individuals and of the world around them, through experiences in improvised drama. Classes, organized throughout the city, are concentrated in culturally disadvantaged areas. The author feels drama holds promises for the unmotivated, the reluctant, and the nonreader.

14. Field, C. W. "Creative Dramatics in Philadelphia," *Wilson Library Bulletin* 40 (December 1965): 344. The author encourages children to observe the world around them through their senses, and then to *use* what they have experienced in their role playing; she feels this stimulates their imagination even further. She also believes drama involves sense memory, emotion memory, characterization, and communication.

15. Hayes, Eloise. "Expanding the Child's World Through Drama and Movement," *Childhood Education* 47 (April 1971): 360–367. Hayes describes in detail the work of an Hawaiian fifth-grade teacher, including an analysis of the lesson sequence she uses. The article recommends teacher participation and gives concrete suggestions for avoiding discipline problems.

16. Heathcote, Dorothy. "How Does Drama Serve Thinking, Talking and Writing?" *Elementary English* 47 (December 1970): 1077–1081. The author discusses two aspects of drama: creative work and coping work. Other considerations are five relevant areas which require consideration in drama, the teacher's

role in drama, and specific suggestions about how to make drama work in the classroom.

17. Hentoff, Nat. "Among the Wild Things," *The New Yorker* 49 (January 22, 1966): 39ff. A fascinating "inside look" at the captivating author of *Where the Wild Things Are, Nutshell Library,* and the illustrator of such works as *The Bat Poet* (by Randall Jarrell) and *A Hole is to Dig* (by Ruth Krauss). This exceptionally creative person has done many books of use for drama leaders.

18. Karioth, J., "Creative Dramatics As An Aid in Developing Creative Thinking Abilities," *Speech Teacher* 19 (November 1970): 301–309. This scientific study, using the Torrance Tests of Creative Thinking, is of special interest to teachers of inner-city children, though the small number of subjects in the experiment is a limitation. The attention paid to factors in the classroom environment is unusual.

19. Klingsick, Judith. "Ideas in Motion Youth Theater: A Growing Expression of Creativity," *Young Children* 23 (September 1968): 324–328. An anecdotal report of the attempts made at Trinity University to encourage the development of children's creativity through drama. Klingsick describes the basic elements of drama to which children are exposed in the program.

20. Merow, Erva Loomis. "Every Child on Stage," *Instructor* 79 (June 1970): 36–39. Merow reports on a summer enrichment program in drama for children in grades one through six. Emphasis is on the teacher participating, in order to build students' confidence. The project involved music, some puppetry, and culminated with a film made by the children.

21. NCTE/ERIC Report. "Oral Dramatics Approach to Teaching English," *English Journal* 58 (April 1969): 614–621. The article is concerned with the uses of both creative dramatics and choral speaking with children and points out the uses of each, especially in introducing poetry to students. It identifies the area of problem solving as one especially affected through the use of dramatics.

22. Oster, Gwen. "Structure in Creativity," *Elementary English* 46 (April 1969): 438–443. This is an attempt to identify some of the specific skills students may develop which can help structure drama experiences. Oster points out with clarity the difference between structure which frees and one which completely lacks control. She makes a sound argument for developing a sequence of skills to be taught to children.

23. Pitcole, Marcia. "Black Boy and Role Playing: A Scenario for Reading Success," *English Journal* 57 (November 1968): 1140–1142. The author uses role playing to motivate interest in reading. She has children dramatize the more explosive scenes from books, which leads the children to become interested in reading more of the book.

24. Reich, Rosalyn. "Puppetry—A Language Tool," *Exceptional Children* 34 (April 1968): 621–623. This article deals with the use of puppetry in a language program for visually handicapped children in a depressed urban area. A measurable improvement in oral language was noted as a result of the experience.

25. Royce, Elizabeth S. "The Play is the Thing," *New York State Education* 54 (January 1967): 41–43. In this article the author presents the idea that formal casting for parts in a play can provide children with an experience leading to "socially acceptable outlets for aggressions." The idea of a formal play is different than that usually advocated by improvised drama leaders, so the article provides a helpful contrast to other material recommended.

26. Shaw, Ann M. "A Taxonomical Study of the Nature and Behavioral Objectives of Creative Drama," *Educational Theatre Journal* 22 (December 1970): 361–372. This study is interesting because it represents the first large-scale attempt to systematize the objectives of drama, following Bloom's *Taxonomy of Educational Objectives Handbook I: Cognitive Domain*. While some may object to such a structured approach to drama, the organization makes it possible to examine analytically some drama components which are often ignored.

27. Side, Ronald. "Creative Drama," *Elementary English* 46 (April 1969): 431–435. Side views drama as an important phase of oral expression and as a good method for encouraging creativity. He stresses the importance of concentration, imagination, use of the senses, voice, and the emotions.

28. Siks, Geraldine. "An Appraisal of Creative Dramatics," *Educational Theatre Journal* 17, no. 4 (December 1965): 328–334. Siks' provides a comprehensive summary of the growth of the drama movement, begun in 1924 by Winifred Ward. She examines the books, other printed materials, and the courses offered by colleges. She includes a comprehensive bibliography and some helpful definitions by a variety of people. Siks' conclusion is that, unfortunately, drama ". . . remains a peripheral rather than a central subject of study."

29. Wagner, Guy. "What Schools Are Doing: Creative Dramatics," *Education* 80 (January 1960): 317. Wagner feels that this dynamic activity contributes favorably to the major purposes of language arts, leading to ease and clarity of expression. It also releases children's energy and emotions while exposing incorrect concepts.

30. Weisheit, Marilyn. "Knowing is Experiencing," *Childhood Education* 44 (April 1968): 498–500. This article relates the experience of a kindergarten teacher using egg-hatching as motivation for a creative dramatics experience. Children pantomimed and developed a story on the basis of their observations.

31. Woods, Margaret S. "Learning Through Creative Dramatics," *Educational Leadership* 18 (October 1960): 18–23. Woods points out that a child creates his own forms, and a full self-realization develops as the child becomes involved in the thinking, feeling, and experiencing which make up dramatics. She also states her belief that such experiences promote a capacity for coping with problems.

32. Zinsmaster, Wanna M. "Contributions of Creative Dramatics to Teaching Social Studies," *Speech Teacher* 14 (November 1965): 305. The author feels that this technique can give social studies an air of reality, as children explore the possible thoughts and feelings of other people, rather than simply learn factual information about them. She also states that dramatics allows children to share in the thinking and action of people of many times and places.

List Four

Because this book considers spontaneous dramatics as one of the language arts, much use is made of literature as motivation. Not all drama leaders rely this heavily on literary materials, but certainly this is one of the richest and most accessible sources of ideas for dramatics. Again, in this list the attempt is not to be comprehensive, but rather to include those materials which I have found to be of help in working with children.

If there is a problem in using literature in dramatics, it is: there is so much literature that making choices is difficult. Often, too, the teacher may know about a story, perhaps even remember one—or a child might suggest one—but she may not know how to locate it. The *Index to Fairy Tales, Myths and Legends* by Mary Huse Eastman is of much help in locating particular stories for which you are searching. Published by Faxton Company (Boston, 1926), it has two supplements (1937 and 1952), and this convenient reference tool makes it possible to find virtually any of the pieces of literature you might need to use. Similarly, it is a valuable tool in locating several versions of the same story when you are working with the idea of variation on a theme in literature.

1. Bulfinch, Thomas. *A Book of Myths,* ill. H. Sewell. New York: MacMillan, 1942. The delightful aspect of this edition is that it uses versions of the myths different from those usually included in anthologies. One could use these to good advantage as contrasts to the more "standard" versions usually found in books. The book includes the Midas Touch myth. You should be aware that both myths and legends are somewhat more difficult to use, simply because fewer clues are included in them, and children will need to create more from the few leads within the material. For example, there is little indication of physical detail, dialogue, or personal points of view in either of these forms. This does not mean that they shouldn't be used, but rather that the leader will need to work harder at drawing ideas for playing from the children.

2. Fransconi, Antonio. *The Snow and the Sun.* New York: Harcourt Brace Jovanovich, 1961. As a drama leader you might be interested in using this South American folk rhyme with its cumulative refrain as a motivation for drama activities. The powerful woodcuts, growing in intensity, provide a compelling visual stimulus. Children react positively to the conflicts described between the snow, water, wind, and other elements, and the animal and human participants in the primitive tale.

3. Grimm, The Brothers. "The Fisherman and His Wife." Of the many versions which are available of these old tales, I have found two to be most appealing. The Brothers Grimm, *Household Stories* (Ann Arbor: Zerox, 1966) is a facsimilie of the 1882 version with pictures by Walter Crane. It's rare treat as the pictures seem so appropriate, but one which children will need to be taught

to enjoy. The other, also to be treasured for its illustrations, is completely different. *Grimm's Fairy Tales* (Chicago: Follett Publishing 1968) contains an introduction by Frances Clarke Sayers and an absolutely first-rate collection of full-color reproductions of paintings done by children.

As mentioned in Chapter 2, this is an excellent story to use in developing a sense of conflict as a dramatic element. The fisherman, who is the tragic figure, is caught between his termagant wife and the fish. The reversal of fortunes at the end is particularly effective. The characterization of the wife, particularly her greedy desire to be king (instead of queen), is a strong one. Leaders might find using *Four Sea Interludes* by Benjamin Britten (London #18354) helpful.

4. Lang, Andrew. *The Green Fairy Book.* Originally published by Longmans Green and Company (London, 1956), this series of books with different color names (e.g., Blue Fairy Book, Red Fairy Book, etc.), have recently been reissued in paperback format by Dover Publications. They are an invaluable source of fairy tales, particularly of the more unfamiliar ones.

5. Simon, Mina and Howard Simon. *If You were an Eel, How Would You Feel?* Chicago: Follett Publishing, 1963. A good book to use in beginning animal movement with children, it explores several animals' activities and evokes their feelings while doing these.

6. Small, Ernest. *Baba Yaga.* Boston: Houghton Mifflin, 1966. Children are charmed by the incongruities which pervade this old Russian folk tale set in the "darkest part of the forest." Marusia's encounters with the witch in her chicken-footed house and the articulate hedgehog who turns into Dmitri lend themselves well to use in drama. Many other adventures grow quickly out of the bare outline provided by Small and illustrated so captivatingly by Blair Lent. "Where else did they sail in the mortar?" is a question which opens endless possibilities.

7. Sperry, Armstrong. *Call It Courage.* New York: MacMillan, 1940. Middle-grade children, boys especially, will be enthralled with the story of Mafatu, the Polynesian boy, whose battle with his enemy, the sea, ended in victory. Illustrative of the conflict of man competing with a force larger than himself, the story provides many opportunities for dramatization. Longer than some other materials included here, it should probably be done in several sessions.

8. Thurber, James. *Many Moons.* New York: Harcourt Brace Jovanovich, 1943. The dilemma posed by Princess Lenore's illness, caused by a surfeit of raspberry tarts, is one which many children delight in trying to solve. They will come up with solutions to the problem much more ingenious than those of the court magician, high chamberlain, and wizard. Children can empathize with the wily jester and develop other episodes involving the "cast" of characters.

List Five

In dramatics, as in other good teaching, variety is crucial, and the drama leader will often use aural stimulus as a change of pace. The recordings listed on the next page have served as motivation for children of all ages. You would probably find some of them helpful with your group.

154 *Reference Lists*

1. Barlin, Anne and Paul Barlin. *The Art of Learning Through Movement.* Los Angeles: The Ward Ritchie Press, 1971. One of the freshest sets of materials to come along, this combination book and records by the Barlins, who are dancers, is designed to make it possible for all teachers to provide experiences in rhythmic movement for children. Clearly explained, lavishly illustrated, and featuring an eye-pleasing format, this creative book provides many ideas which could develop from movement into more extended drama experiences.

2. Holloway, Stanley. *The Elephant Alphabet.* Riverside Records #1415. A charming evocation of animals, skillfully read it should be of use in getting children to respond rhythmically. You could use it to correlate activities in drama with other language arts, when young children are enjoying the myriad of alphabet books.

3. *Mother Goose* (Including the voices of Cyril Richard, Celeste Holme, and Boris Karloff). Caedmon Records, T.C. #1091. This is an especially valuable record to use in talking about voice qualities and characterization. It is a wonderfully fanciful demonstration of the success vocally talented people have in changing their voices to evoke different characters.

After listening to it, you might encourage children to try reading some of the same rhymes, experimenting with changing their voices. Or, you might use some of the rhymes to build understanding of characterization, by having children improvise new story lines for the rhyme.

Though the Mother Goose rhymes are generally thought of as primarily intended for younger children, you will find them to be effective when used as motivation for character development—even with intermediate-grade children.

4. Potter, Beatrix. *Tales of Peter Rabbit.* Wonderland Records (division of Riverside, RLP) #1434. There is a no more effective way of capturing children's interest than to share with them some of the enchanting works of Miss Potter. This record, read so competently by Vivian Leigh, is one of the best available.

Most of the above have been of use primarily to motivate children to do *interpretive* movement, i.e., to move like something real. Another kind of movement is *abstract* movement, in which the child does not try to move like something, but rather moves his body in the ways the music makes him feel. Several leaders have found march music a good way to begin doing rhythmic movement with children. The simple rhythmic ideas and repetition with variation evoke a response even from kindergarten-age children. You might try using the *Stars and Stripes Forever,* or other Sousa marches. See, for example, Everest #3280, *John Phillip Sousa Conducts His Own Marches.* Others good to use include:

5. Prokofieff, Serge. *Peter and the Wolf.* Vanguard, SRV #174SD. Though the story is in itself probably too extended for use as is, it makes an excellent motivation for dramatics when some scenes from it are used with children. You might also find *The Lt. Kije Suite* (Columbia #13292) useful, particularly with

children between eight and fourteen. These older children respond freely to the vigorous rhythms in this piece.

6. Saint-Saens, Camille. *Carnival of the Animals.* Angel #35135. This is another of several program music pieces which are good motivation for rhythmic movement. Children can listen to the evocative sections of this and improvise animal movements suggested by the music.

List Six

There are many films of interest to the spontaneous dramatics leader; most of these serve to further his understanding of the art form, but some can be used to stimulate children.

Where do you go for lists of films, especially if you are not teaching near a film distribution center? Probably the single most helpful source for locating films is the *Index to Sixteen Millimeter Educational Films,* (New York: R. R. Bowker Company, 1969), a very comprehensive, easy-to-read, and simple-to-use annotated bibliography of films. The type is clear, indexing is understandable, and the organization is helpful.

1. *Another Way of Saying It,* Kindergarten Videotape Series. WHA–TV, 3313 University Avenue, Madison, Wisconsin 53706. 20 minutes each. Program #18. This is a delightful series of programs for use with kindergarten children. Program #18 is concerned with gestures; another program deals with the many versions of the same folk tale.

2. *Basic Movement Education in England.* University of Michigan, Audio-Visual Education Center, Ann Arbor, Michigan, 48103. 19 minutes, black and white, sound. This film presents a problem-solving approach to the study and refinement of body movement through space. It stresses individual approach rather than formal lessons and shows various age groups demonstrating rhythm and movement.

3. *Building Children's Personality with Creative Dancing.* Bailey Films, 6509 Delongpre Ave., Hollywood, California, 90028. 30 minutes, color, sound. In teaching dancing to a group of boys and girls, the teacher skillfully guides each child toward a unique personal and improvised style, praising him all the way. The movie follows a child from his point of embarrassment and tenseness to his eventual demonstration of creative expression.

4. *Dance Your Own Way.* Bailey Films, 6509 Delongpre Ave., Hollywood, California, 90028. 10 minutes, color, sound. Children listen to a record and dance their own way, sometimes with the group, sometimes alone to a rhythm they alone see and hear.

5. *Ideas and Me.* Dallas Theatre Center, 3636 Turtle Creek Blvd., Dallas, Texas, 75200. 17 minutes, color. This film traces the growth and personal development of a group of children as they participate in all aspects of creative

theater. It culminates with excerpts from the group's own version of a Greek tragedy.

6. *Illusions.* Center for Mass Communications, Columbia University Press, 562 W. 113th St., New York, N.Y., 10025. 15 minutes, black and white. A superb film to use in introducing pantomime to children. The mime begins with very small motions of the head, which gradually enlarge to include the entire body. Mimes of wheels, a rope climb, tug-of-war, and walking are included. The animal mimes, a chicken and monkey, are especially noteworthy because they are so free of stereotyped movement. The film ends with a longer episode featuring a lion tamer.

7. *Improvised Drama,* Parts One and Two. Time-Life Films, 43 West 16th St. New York, N.Y., 10011. 30 minutes, black and white, sound. Of use in helping you to understand the range of possibilities in drama, these two films show a distinguished English drama leader, John Hodgson, working with teenage children. The improvised dramas they evolve are based on conflict situations.

8. *Just Imagine.* (Kinescope). Indiana University, Audio-Visual Center, Bloomington, Indiana, 47401. 15 minutes, black and white, sound. Students present an orientation to techniques for developing creative dramatics by rummaging through an old trunk and creating characterizations.

9. *The Mime.* Center for Mass Communications, Columbia University Press, 562 W. 113th St., New York, N.Y. 10025. 29 minutes, black and white. A film designed for adults, this is divided into three segments: 1) it shows the training necessary for mime, 2) the mime discusses his personal views on the topic, and 3) it shows him getting ready for a performance. In addition to the mime himself, the film shows several students at work.

10. *Mother Tongue,* Part 5—"The Sensitive Tool." Time-Life Films, 43 W. 16th St., New York, N.Y., 10011. 20 minutes, black and white, sound. This sensitively done series, originally created for BBC-TV, explores many aspects of the newly popular British Infant School Movement. This last segment, which shows children at "the top end of the school," illustrates how bodily movement (in this case to Moussorgsky's Night on Bald Mountain) can lead into poetry and prose writing.

11. "Movement in Time and Space," Segment 6 in *Discovery and Experience.* Time-Life Films, 43 W. 16th St., New York, N.Y., 10011. 30 minutes, black and white. Produced originally for BBC-TV, this series is filmed on location in a number of British infant schools. In this segment the teacher is promoting activity in drama and dance, so that bodily movement expresses what is in the children's minds. The children work both singly and in groups, sometimes moving to music, sometimes adding dialogue.

12. *Movement Education.* State University of Iowa, Bureau of Audio-Visual Instruction, Iowa City, Iowa, 50010. Black and white, sound. This series of four films deals with children exploring space and time, problem solving in dance, and creation of dance using the inspiration of music.

13. *Pantomime.* Dallas Theatre Center, 3636 Turtle Creek Blvd., Dallas, Texas, 75200. 21 minutes, black and white. This film, using adult pantomimes, skillfully blends classic pantomime technique and the modern dance idiom in six episodes, with various emotional contexts.

14. *Pantomime for the Actor.* S-L Film Productions, 5126 Hartwick St., Los Angeles, California 90041. 20 minutes, color, sound. Earl Lewin, pantomime artist, demonstrates the implications of pantomime to the beginning actor. He shows how it is used to convey emotion, action, character, setting, and plot.

15. *Rainshower.* Churchill Films, 6671 Sunset Blvd., Los Angeles, Calif., 90028. 15 minutes, color, sound. This is a lyric evocation of the progress of a storm, from the first few drops which startles a hen in the parched barnyard to the pounding torrent on the quickly deserted city street. It offers many opportunities for improvisation based on ideas in the film, or only suggested by it.

16. *Sketches.* Center for Mass Communications, Columbia University Press, 562 W. 113th St., New York, N.Y. 10025. 16 minutes, black and white. This film, a companion to *Illusions,* deals with more sophisticated topics than does the other film. The mime presents: an athlete, games, a sculptor, and a nightmare. Of interest primarily to the teacher, this film is effective in developing an understanding of mime as an art form.

List Seven

The leader will often make use of poetry as motivation for drama. With their abbreviated forms, succinct statements, and frequent singular viewpoints, poems can often be used in their entirety. They seldom require condensing or telescoping, in order to make them usable.

How do you find a poem? A particularly invaluable reference is *Index to Children's Poetry* by John E. and Sara W. Brewton (New York: H. W. Wilson, 1942. 1st Supp., 1957, 2nd Supp., 1965). Arranged by topic, title, first line, and author, this set of books allows you to locate virtually any poem which has been published, despite your fragmentary knowledge about it.

1. "Mice" by Rose Fyleman. Association for Childhood Education, *Sung Under the Silver Umbrella* (New York: MacMillan, 1939), p. 67. A particularly effective poem to use, it sets up the question: What is *your* reaction (and is it the same as mine) to the first two lines of the poem? It makes good use of visual, auditory, and kinesthetic images, as well as motion, all of which are consciously manipulated to create a positive attitude toward the subject. Children have a sense of kinship and can respond to the poem as a motivation for dramatics.

2. "The Little Clown Puppet" by Carolyn Haywood. Sara and John E. Brewton, *Bridled with Rainbows* (New York: MacMillan, 1952), p. 32. This poem

is effective to use in getting children to consider movement, particularly that of a marionette. The adventures which befall the little clown after he is picked up by the crow capture children's interest. They especially delight in devising other endings for the poem.

The anthology by the Brewtons, including poems by Rachel Field, David McCord, Amy Lowell, Walter de la Mare, Rose Fyleman, and Robert Louis Stevenson, among others, is divided into categories ranging from "Off to Somewhere" to "A Little House Will Please."

3. "The House with Nobody in It" by Joyce Kilmer. Blanche J. Thomson, *Silver Pennies* (New York: MacMillan, 1956), p. 15. Using this poem with children will evoke a wide variety of responses to the question: Who *was* there? (Use just the first stanza—the rest is bad poetry). There are many playable incidents to be developed by exploring ideas concerning *why* the house was tragic, what was the nature of the tragedy, and what were the causes of it.

The anthology contains the work of Hilda Conkling, Sara Teasdale, Robert Frost, and Carl Sandburg, among other poets, all of which are of use with children.

4. "Richard Cory" by Edwin A. Robinson. Included in *Modern American Poetry* (New York: Harcourt Brace Jovanovich, 1950), p. 123. Undoubtedly of use exclusively with older children, the poem is one of those pieces made effective by the complete shock of the last line, which destroys the image created before then. Sixth-grade children will be able to handle the problem presented in this poem and will gain strength from confronting the issue it raises. It is particularly helpful to contradict the idea that in dramatics everything is "sweetness and light."[1]

The anthology, though not intended specifically for children, includes some fine poems by Walt Whitman, James Weldon Johnson, Santayana, and Vachel Lindsay, which would be useful in drama.

In working with animals as motivation, the leader sometimes uses several poems about the same subject, to enrich the child's concept of the animal. In working with the idea of cats, as an example, you could use as motivation:

1. "The Cat" by Mary Britton Miller[2]
2. "The Housecat" by Annette Wynne[3]
3. "Fog" by Carl Sandburg[4]
4. *Old Possum's Practical Book of Cats* by T.S. Elliott[5] (Available on Argo Records, R.G., #116).

---

[1]With older children it would be especially effective to use the Simon and Garfunkel recording using these words, included in *Sounds of Silence* (Columbia #CS9269).
[2]Included in Arbuthnot, op. cit., p. 50.
[3]Included in Huber, op. cit., p. 127.
[4]Included in Arbutnot, op. cit., p. 161
[5]T.S. Elliott, *Old Possums Practical Book of Cats* (Harcourt Brace Jovanovich, 0000).

Sometimes teachers use the poems of other children, rather than adult poets, to motivate children. "A Cat," included in the book *Miracles,*[6] would be appropriate here.

List Eight

In a world becoming increasingly more visually oriented, the drama leader needs to be aware of the variety of materials available to him which he can use for drama sessions. Some of these are described below.

One drama leader has experienced good success with using a tree silhouette projected on an overhead projector. He uses such questions as, "Can you grow as this tree would grow?" "Where might a tree with this shape grow?" and "What sort of animals might you expect would live in an area with trees like this?"

You can make good use of the color title slides available, for instance, from *Title Specialties* (Box 247, Birdsboro, Pennsylvania, 19508, set of six assorted colors, $1.00). These slides, available at most photography supply houses, are colored, but without design or lettering. You can draw on them with inks or felt pens, and can apply designs to them with paints or Zip-Tone,* then project these on a screen for children to see and respond to.

The book *Masks and Mask Makers* by Kari Hunt and Bernice Wells Carlson (New York: Abingdon Press, 1961) is invaluable for evoking responses from children, who are delighted by the unusual masks illustrated in the book. Project one of these in an opaque projector, with the room suitably dark to establish the mood, and you will find children can respond freely.

1. *Family of Man,* ed. Edward Steichen. New York: New American Library (Signet). An older book, this is nevertheless useful to a leader in developing characterization. The people in these photographs vary in age, status, and country of origin, which adds to the book's usefulness. Almost any of them could be a good springboard into a drama session.

2. "The Urban Education Series," ed. Betty Atwell Wright. New York: John Day, 1967. This is a particularly fine series of large picture books (18" by 18"), unique and of much value to leaders working with children from "disadvantaged" urban environments. Either the city volumes (eight separate ones dealing with metropolitan areas, like Chicago and New York) or the particular

---

[6]Richard Lewis, *Miracles* (New York: Simon and Schuster, 1966), p. 102. Teachers who do not as yet know about this sensitive volume of poetry by children from many countries will be impressed by the variety and insight the poems show and by the visual sophistication of the book's format. Lewis is a good name to know; his other collections of children's work are equally distinguished.

*Sheets of transparent color, with clear adhesive backing, available in art supply stores.

content volumes (for example, *Growing Is* ..., *A Family Is* ..., *A Neighbor Is* ...) would be very useful for stimulating dramatics.

3. "Modern Art Series" by The Instructor Publication Inc., Subsidiary of Harcourt Brace and Jovanovich, N.Y. Another valuable means of motivating children to respond in dramatics, these large (12 ¾" by 16") full-color reproductions range in time from Degas to Motherwell and include a wide variety of subjects. The Toulouse-Lautrec circus painting, for example, is only one of the many included which work well as drama motivation. The format of the series, with each reproduction mounted separately on a heavy cardboard folder, makes presentation simple and adds to the durability of the materials.

Summary

The materials listed in this chapter can be considered no more than an indication of the range of possibilities which exist. As you work with children you will find different categories of materials which work well for you, and you will find new materials to put into the categories we have considered here, for ideas, materials, procedures, and outcomes are always changing. What is included here has worked for me. What will be included in your list after a few years of working in dramatics with children will be much different. What is *most* desirable is that your program with children will remain always truly a program of spontaneous dramatics—an experience in creating for children *and* one important aspect of the language arts.

Index

Achille's Heel Myth, 45
Actions, 85, 86
   pantomime, 93-94
   units of, 124, 135
Adventures of Tom Sawyer, 99
Alice's Adventures in Wonderland, 7-8
Allen, H., 35
Andrews, G., 60, 61, 90
Animal poems, list of, 158
"April Rain Song," 49, 51
Arbuthnot's Anthology of Children's Literature, 22, 107, 123, 134
Art for Primary Grades, 111
Asbjornsen, P.C., 107
Austin, M., 90, 115, 118

Baranski, M., 129
Barnfield, G., 2, 55, 61, 64
Beauty and the Beast, 79
Behavioral objectives, 78
Behind the Waterfall, 96
Blank, W. E., 27, 28
Body, use of in drama, 60, 61 (*see also* Kinesics)
Body Language, 90
Book of Witches, A, 96
Books, list of, 144-46
Brave White Bear of the North, 95
Brown, K. L., 75, 76

Carlson, B.W., 129
Character expansion, 82, 141
Characterization, 52, 109, 123-25, 126-28, 132, 135, 136-37
   three aspects of, 80-82
   three qualities of, 63-64
Cinderella, 11, 79, 83
Clements, H. M., 44
Clements, R. D., 44
"Cloud Shadows," 95
Cole, N. R., 3
Conflict, as element of drama, 103
   lines, 87
   three types of, 62
Creative Drama: The First Steps, 90
Creative dramatics, 5, 14
Creative writing, 98-99
Crist, R. 11, 31, 60, 90, 91, 95
Cullum, A., 29, 30
Culture, study of other peoples, 129

Davidson, D., 76
Davis, D. C., 29
DeAngeli, M., 88
Departure points, sequence of, 101-142
Dialects, 88
Dialogue, 64-66, 126, 132, 138-39
Discussion and questioning, 5, 18-19, 21

161

Index

Drama
  analytical and direct approaches to, 60-62
  components of, 4-5
  formal and informal, compared, 13
  lack of emphasis on, 77-78
  nonverbal elements of, 89-95
  three elements of, 62-66
  values of, 12-15, 77
  (see also Spontaneous drama)
Drama goals, 103
Drama leader, 7
  characteristics of, 40
  ability to listen, 42-44
  ability to question, 44
  belief in drama, 47-49
  flexibility, 41-42, 43
  material selection, 49-51
  role in drama session, 54-57

Emotional stability, 14
Enright, E., 82
Evaluation
  concurrent, 20
  in drama experience, 5
  of drama session, 67-68
  terminal, 20-21

Fast, J., 90
Ferris, S. R., 32, 35
Films, list of, 155-57
Fingerpaintings, 111-12
"Fishing Trip," 95
Flagg, A., 33
"Fox and the Grapes, The," 9

"Galoshes," 50-51
Ginger Bread Boy, 66
Goldilock and the Three Bears, 24, 82, 83
Group evaluation, 20, 68
Group goals, 103

Hallock, G., 25
Hansel and Gretel, 84
Harriet the Spy, 85

"Heath-Cat, The," 16
Heinrich, J. S., 58
Henry, M., 88
"Hippopotamus, The," 89
Holt, J., 59
Honesty, 68-69
Hunt, K., 129, 159

"I Know a Place," 95
Impressional treatment, 29
Improvisation, 8-10, 37, 41, 42, 53, 66-67, 91, 126, 128, 131
  and literature, 84, 85
  and reading, 79-84
Index to Children's Poetry, 157
Index to Fairy Tales, Myths, and Legends, 152
Index to Sixteen Millimeter Educational Films, 155
Instructor magazine, 75
Interpretation, 8-10, 79, 104, 107

Jack and the Beanstalk, 66, 84
Juncture, in language, 31, 32, 33, 87

Keats, E. J., 86
Kinesics, 32, 34-35, 89-94
King of Hearts, The, 52
King with Six Friends, 1
"Kites," 95
"Knapsack, The," 81
Kuhn, W., 17

Leavitt, H. D., 17
Lefevre, C. A., 34
Lenski, L., 82, 88
Lessons (sessions), 7-8
Lewis, C. D., 31
Listening, 4
  ability, 42-44, 45
  skills
    basic listening, 96
    evaluative listening, 97
Literature, list of, 152
Literature program and drama, 84-86
Little Miss Muffett, 83

Index

"Little Picture," 95
Little Red Riding Hood, 23, 83
Lofting, H., 120, 126
Loon's Necklace, 129

McIlwain, D. S., 111
Magic Bed-Knob, The, 91, 134-140
Marceau, M., 92
Mask Making, 129
Masks and Mask Makers, 129, 159
Materials, motivational, 5, 10, 16-18, 27, 49-51, 103
  list of, 109
  occassional materials list, 146-47
  treatment of, 51-54
Mehrabian, A., 32, 35, 89
Method, 103
Midas Touch, 9, 27, 45, 84, 88
Moffett, J., 87
Mood, 132, 139
  interpretation, 114, 119
Movement, 85, 90, 104, 111, 117
  abstract, 111-14, 154
  interpretive, 105, 106, 154
  (*see also* Kinesics)
Mrs. Wallaby-Jones, 63
Music, 112-14

National Council of Teachers of English, 28
National Geographic, 129
Norton, M., 91, 134, 142

"Old Mother Hubbard," 36
Opaque projector ideas, 159
Oral composition, 35-38, 86
Oral language, 3-4
  conflict, 87
  dialects, 88
  paralinguistic, 87-88
Oral skills, 76
Oster, G., 78
Owl's Nest, 96

Pandora's Box, 27, 33-34, 89
Pantomime, 5, 19, 78, 91-94
Paralanguage, 31-34, 87

Particularization, 91, 92
Periodical articles, list of, 147-51
Personality factors, 27, 28
Phantom Tollbooth, 86
"Pheasant, The," 89
"Picnic Basket, The," 64
Picture books, list of, 159-60
Pictures, use of, 119-22, 126, 132-34
  mask, 129-32
  mental, 117-18
Pitch, in language, 31, 32, 33, 87
Playing of an idea, 5, 19, 52, 54
Plot extension, 54, 81, 122-32, 134, 136
Poetry, 85, 95
  list of, 157-59
  use of in sequence, 114-19
"Poor Old Lady", 25-26
Potter, B., 65
Praise, 68-69
"Pretending," 95
Problems, physical,
  class size, 69
  scheduling, 71
  space, 69, 71
Puppets, 94
Push Back the Desks, 29
"Puss in Boots," 80

Questioning and discussion, 5, 18-19
Questions, ability to ask, 44-46

Rachmaninoff's *Rhapsody on a Theme of Paganini,* 67
Rainshower, 50
Reading programs and drama, 79-84
Reasoning powers, 15
Recordings, list of, 153-55
Responses, 19, 41, 67
  freedom of, 57-60
Roosevelt Grady, 88
Rhythm, 139

Sanders, N., 45
"Sandhill Crane, The," 10, 22, 61, 90, 115

164 Index

Scene expansion, 142
Schools, and the drama program, 72-73
Senses, use of, 17-19
Seuss, Dr., 63
Shaw, A., 4, 78
Shotwell, L., 88
Siks, G. B., 12, 77
Silberman, C., 77
Sleeping Beauty, 27
"Snakes and Snails," 25
Snow White and the Seven Dwarfts, 27, 83
Social-emotional values of drama, 77
Sohn, D. A., 17
"Some One", 17
Speech, simultaneous, 65
Spontaneous drama
  components of, 16-21
  qualities of, 11-12
    inclusive quality, 22
    on-going quality, 23-24
    process quality, 27
    recurring drama, 24
  as a sequence, 104-105
  sessions, 7-8
"Stone in the Road, The," 35
Stone Soup, 11
Stories to Dramatize, 86
"Story of Mrs. Tubbs," 123
Strawberry Girl, 88
Stress, in language, 31, 32, 33, 87

Subject matter applications for drama, 38, 77, 129

Tales of Peter Rabbit, 65
Teacher evaluation, 20
Teachers (*see* Drama leaders)
Teamwork, social value, 14
Terminology, in dramatics, 5-8
Textbooks and dramatic activities, 75, 76
Theatre, and dramatics, 11
Thee, Hannah, 88
Theraphy, 14
Three Billy Goats Gruff, 32, 96, 107
Title Specialties, 159
Today's Education, 65
Tom Tit Tot, 97
Torrance, E. P., 36

Verbal reinforcement, 56-57
Verbal symbols, paralanguage, 31, 32, 33
Verbs for acting, 51, 85, 90, 104, 116
Visual stimulus, 17, 19
Vocabulary growth, 27, 28-31, 95-96
Voice qualities, 27, 28

Ward, W., 29, 35-36, 86
White Clown (art), 17
"Wind Weather," 46

Get more quickly to characterization

Sit & talk to them more

Frame a unifying question in
        opening session

Select specific material & practice
        making questions to lead them
        into it & beyond it.

Introduce specific exercises to elicit
        dialogue (Strunk - p 65?)

Have only 2 on a team.